THE LAND FLOWING WITH MILK AND HONEY

THE LAND FLOWING WITH MILK AND HONEY

Dr. Jaerock Lee

THE LAND FLOWING WITH MILK AND HONEY
by Dr. Jaerock Lee
Published by Urim Books (Representative: Kyungtae Noh)
73, Yeouidaebang-ro 22-gil, Dongjak-Gu, Seoul, Korea
www.urimbooks.com

All rights reserved. This book or parts thereof may not be reproduced in any form, stored in a retrieval system, or transmitted in any form or by any means, electronic, mechanical, photocopying, recording or otherwise, without prior written permission of the publisher.

Unless otherwise noted, all Scripture quotations are taken from the Holy Bible, NEW AMERICAN STANDARD BIBLE, ®, Copyright © 1960, 1962, 1963, 1968, 1971, 1972, 1973, 1975, 1977, 1995 by The Lockman Foundation. Used by permission.

Copyright © 2009 by Dr. Jaerock Lee
ISBN: 978-89-7557-234-0
Translated by Dr. Esther K. Chung. Used by permission.

Previously published in Korean by Urim Books, Seoul, Korea.
Copyright © 2007 by Dr. Jaerock Lee

First Edition July 2009
  2nd Printing August 2009

Edited by Dr. Geumsun Vin
Designed by Editorial Bureau of Urim Books
Printed by Yewon Printing Company
For more information contact at urimbook@hotmail.com

Prologue

History books that write about the historical facts of a nation often become good guides for the people in later generations. Also novels based on historical facts are loved by the many. I also learned about the wars, collaboration, strategies of different people, and their attitudes of the heart by reading the Chinese classical novel *Romance of the Three Kingdoms*.

But the greatest and best historical record and guide to our lives is the Bible. From the creation of the world to the things that will take place in the future, the Bible contains human history from beginning to end.

God chose the people of Israel and made them a model of human cultivation. He still shows them His love to guide them to the beautiful kingdom of heaven. Especially, the records about the conquest of the Canaan Land written in the five books of Exodus, Leviticus, Numbers, Deuteronomy, and Joshua contain the endless love of God and His earnest desire for us to become holy and sanctified.

The leader of the Exodus, Moses, and his successor, Joshua, both believed in the almighty God. They followed the will of God and showed amazing signs and wonders. They glorified God with the victories they achieved. The opposite is true of the Pharaoh and his ministers who did not accept the Creator God. Instead of accepting Him, they opposed Him. In the end, they faced calamities and curses.

God is truly the Master of history who controls the life, death, fortune, and misfortune of individuals as well as the rise and fall of the nations.

But what is the reason the Canaan Land is called the land flowing with milk and honey?

Genesis 10:19 says, *"The territory of the Canaanite extended from Sidon as you go toward Gerar, as far as Gaza; as you go toward Sodom and Gomorrah and Admah and Zeboiim, as far as Lasha."* The Canaan Land was all of the land that was west of the Jordan River.

Today, it's called 'Palestine.' Unlike the wilderness of Egypt, it had an abundance of water and fertile land. The flocks could produce milk and the land bloomed with flowers so that people could get honey. There were also some barren land, but there were plains in many places. With the mild climate, there were olives, grapes, pomegranates, figs, and rye. The area also had many cattle and abundant seafood.

The Canaan Land is also the Promised Land of God (Deuteronomy 11:9), and spiritually, it symbolizes the kingdom of heaven that we are longing to possess. The process of the Israelites relying on the promise of God and conquering the land flowing with milk and honey symbolically represents the spiritual battle that we face in our Christian lives.

When we look into the process of the Exodus, the forty years in the wilderness, crossing the Jordan River and conquering the city of Jericho and then the Land of Canaan, we can see the life's journey of receiving salvation and marching towards the kingdom of heaven.

God brought the Israelites out of Egypt and guided them to the Canaan Land flowing with milk and honey. Likewise, He wants everyone to have true faith and enjoy eternal rest in the beautiful heavenly kingdom. Furthermore, He wants every one of us to have faith that pleases God so that we can receive answers to whatever we ask and do all things by His power.

This book *The Land Flowing with Milk and Honey* retraces the steps of Moses and Joshua, as they marched on with only faith and belief in the promise of God. I believe the readers will receive the blessings and learn about the secrets of receiving answers and blessings. They will also be able to realize the importance of seemingly trivial things in every day life.

I pray in the name of the Lord that the readers will believe all the promises of God, conquer the Canaan Land flowing with milk and honey, and by force take hold of the city of New Jerusalem, the best dwelling place of the heavenly kingdom.

Lastly, I give thanks to Dr. Geumsun Vin, Director of Editorial Bureau, Manmin Central Church, and the workers there, and Rev. Joong-won Lee for their dedications, and to everybody who prayed for this work.

Jaerock Lee

Table of Contents

Prologue

Chapter 1   "Bring My People Up from the Land"   · 1
— God Calls Moses

Chapter 2   "I Will Make You as God"   · 23
— Ten Plagues

Chapter 3   "You Shall Know that I Am the LORD Your God"   · 43
— The Exodus

| Chapter 4 | "If the LORD Is Pleased with Us" | · 71 |

– Confession of Joshua and Caleb

| Chapter 5 | "The LORD Your God Is with You" | · 93 |

– The Successor to Moses

| Chapter 6 | They Cross the Jordan on Dry Ground | · 109 |

– Jordan River Stops

Table of Contents

Chapter 7   "The LORD Has Given You the City"   · 125
     – The Conquest of Jericho

Chapter 8   "They Have Transgressed My Covenant"   · 139
     – The Sin of Achan

Chapter 9   The Sun and the Moon Stand Still   · 153
     – Victory of the Battle of Gibeon

Chapter 10   "Give Me This Hill Country"   · 169

    – Devotion of Caleb

Chapter 11   "It Shall Be Yours"   · 181

    – Distribution of the Canaan Land

Chapter 12   "As for Me and My House,
We Will Serve the LORD"   · 193

    – The Last Will of Joshua

Epilogue   – Conquering the Land Flowing with Milk and Honey –

Chapter 1

"Bring My People Up from the Land"

- God Calls Moses -

Exodus 3:7-8

༄༅༔

The LORD said, "I have surely seen the affliction of My people who are in Egypt, and have given heed to their cry because of their taskmasters, for I am aware of their sufferings. So I have come down to deliver them from the power of the Egyptians, and to bring them up from that land to a good and spacious land, to a land flowing with milk and honey."

Today we are living in the 'flood of knowledge and information,' and the computer is one of the main tools that are increasing knowledge and information into higher dimensions. Computers operate according to the programs that have been input.

Likewise, God's providence of 'human cultivation' that has been planned since before time began can be likened to a program; it has been operating until this very day without the slightest error. The people that were chosen to fulfill this providence of God were the Israelites.

Formation of the Nation of Israel

God planned the providence of 'human cultivation' and created the heavens and the earth and everything in the universe to gain true children with whom He could share His true love. God made the first man Adam, walked with him, and gave him the authority to rule over and subdue all things.

Adam and Eve lived in the Garden of Eden for a long period of time. Because they didn't truly understand God's love, they did not keep His word deeply in their hearts.

Consequently they were tempted by the serpent into eating from the tree of the knowledge of good and evil. As a result of that disobedience, they were driven out from the Garden of Eden and had to live by their toil and sweat.

The sins of men only increased; even to the extent that Adam's son, Cain, killed his own brother Abel.

At the time of Noah, the whole world was so full of sins that God even regretted having created men. He finally decided to punish the world. He let Noah, the only righteous man of the time, prepare the ark of salvation, and told him to deliver the message about the punishment.

Nevertheless, people didn't listen to Noah. Finally, every single person on earth except him and his family was punished by water. Amazingly, even Chinese characters have traces of this incident. For example, the character for 'ship' is '船'. This is the combination of 'ark' (舟) with number 'eight' (八), and 'mouth' (口).

> On the very same day Noah and Shem and Ham and Japheth, the sons of Noah, and Noah's wife and the three wives of his sons with them, entered the ark (Genesis 7:13).

This means the eight-member family of Noah went into the ark, because the 'mouth' in Chinese character also refers to 'mouths that eat together,' which means 'family.'

It is a tragedy that mankind fell into death because of Adam's sin, but in another sense it also was in the providence of 'human cultivation.' God chose a righteous man to fulfill this providence. That man is Abraham, who is called the 'father of faith.'

About 4,000 years ago, God established Abraham as the father of faith and gave him the promise that He would give him countless descendants. God called him and brought him out of Ur of the Chaldees (one of the major cities of ancient Mesopotamia), and gave him the Land of Canaan.

> *The LORD said to Abram, after Lot had separated from him, "Now lift up your eyes and look from the place where you are, northward and southward and eastward and westward; for all the land which you see, I will give it to you and to your descendants forever. I will make your descendants as the dust of the earth, so that if anyone can number the dust of the earth, then your descendants can also be numbered. Arise, walk about the land through its length and breadth; for I will give it to you" (Genesis 13:14-17).*

> *And [the LORD] took him outside and said, "Now look toward the heavens, and count the stars, if you are able to count them." And He said to him, "So shall your descendants be" (Genesis 15:5).*

God told Abraham what would happen to his descendants. Namely, God told him that his descendants would be enslaved in Egypt for about 400 years and then they would return to the Land of Canaan.

> *God said to Abram, "Know for certain that your descendants will be strangers in a land that is not theirs, where they will be enslaved and oppressed four hundred years. But I will also judge the nation whom they will serve, and afterward they will come out with many possessions. As for you, you shall go to your fathers in peace; you will be buried at a good old age. Then in the fourth generation they will return here, for the iniquity of the Amorite is not yet complete" (Genesis 15:13-16).*

Abraham gave birth to his son Isaac at the age of one hundred. Isaac begot Esau and Jacob. Esau had the birthright to receive God's blessings as the first son, but he was so hungry that he sold the birthright to his younger brother Jacob for a bowl of lentil stew (Genesis 25:30-34).

To sell the birthright is not something trivial. It proves that Esau had little regard for the blessings for the first son and he also did not believe in God who controls everything. God gives us this warning so that we will not be as one of the immoral or godless like Esau who did not want spiritual blessings and neglected the birthright.

> *There be no immoral or godless person like Esau, who sold his own birthright for a single meal (Hebrews 12:16).*

On the contrary, his brother Jacob longed for spiritual blessings and took hold of them even by force. He was crafty enough to deceive his father Isaac and receive the blessings of the first son. But his heart that longed for spiritual blessing was more proper in God's sight.

God planned to fulfill His providence through the descendants of Jacob and refined him for a long period of time.

Jacob left his home for twenty years, running away from his angry brother, and he realized that he couldn't do anything with his own strength and plans.

His self-righteousness was broken completely and he changed into a kind of person that God desired. He received the new name, 'Israel,' and he had twelve sons who formed the twelve tribes of Israel. The descendants of the tribe of Judah are the Jews who have reestablished Israel today.

> *God said to him, "Your name is Jacob; you shall no longer be called Jacob, but Israel shall be your name." Thus He called him Israel. God also said to him, "I am God Almighty; be fruitful and multiply; a nation and a company of nations shall come from you, and kings shall come forth from you. The land which I gave to Abraham*

and Isaac, I will give it to you, and I will give the land to your descendants after you" (Genesis 35:10-12).

How Did Israelites Come to Stay in Egypt?

Then, why did God permit the people of Israel to go through suffering for 400 years in Egypt?

Let me give you an example. Suppose a boy is praying to God to make him the president of his country. It is obvious that God cannot answer this boy's prayer immediately.

God fulfills everything in an orderly manner according to principles. So, He will first guide this boy to have the qualities to be able to become the president. God will guide him to the quickest way to finish his studies and gain various experiences.

Likewise, God gave Abraham the promise that He would make a great nation of his descendants, but a great nation could not be formed immediately.

When Jacob's family went to Egypt, the number of his family members was only seventy. To make this one family a great nation, God used His amazing wisdom.

Until Israel formed a great nation, they had to have strength. If they had increased in number among so many tribal countries, they would have been attacked by those small countries. So, to protect Israel, God chose Egypt.

Egypt had their king from around 3,000 BC and it had

blossomed into a splendid civilization. It has one of the world's longest histories extending from the time of the Mesopotamian civilization.

God arranged for Joseph, the eleventh son of Jacob, to go to Egypt and let him save the country from the seven-year famine that prevailed in the Middle East.

The reason why Joseph was used to fulfill God's providence was because he had a right and proper heart. He had a good inner heart and excellent wisdom sufficient even to be able to perform the great service of saving Egypt.

Joseph was born of Rachel. Since Rachel was the wife whom Jacob loved the most, Jacob showed favoritism toward Joseph. Because of this, Joseph was hated by his brothers, who were sons of other wives. Joseph was hated even more after telling his brothers about his dream. Finally, he was sold into Egypt as a slave to Potiphar, an officer of the Pharaoh.

Joseph left his home and his father and overnight he had become a slave in another country.

But because he trusted God, he didn't fall into immoral conduct or give up on his life. He always did his best in any given situation.

He took care of the possessions of his master as if they were his own, and he was careful and faithful in acting with the heart of the master. He also had the heart to treat his brothers, who had sold him, with goodness (Genesis 45:3-

8). God blessed all things of Potiphar since Joseph was put in charge of all of his master's possessions.

This same principle can be applied in the same way today. Even though we may have difficult problems or situations, if we love God and live by His word, His love and compassion will befall us. We will be acknowledged in our duties and receive blessings.

The most important thing is how much we revere God, act faithfully in all things, and how much we obey the word of God by walking in the path of righteousness.

Joseph faced a big test. When he gained the trust of his master and was put in charge of all his master's possessions in the household, the wife of his master began to tempt him.

He didn't want to commit a sin before God; he also wanted to keep the trust relation with his master. He sternly refused her attempts to seduce him. She then wrongfully accused Joseph that he had forcefully attempted to lie with her. Finally, he was put in the jail where Pharaoh's prisoners were confined.

Joseph was the chosen one to fulfill the providence of God, and why did he have to suffer many difficulties - being sold into another country as a slave, and furthermore being wrongfully accused and sent to jail?

For Joseph to have the ability and qualities to become

the prime minister of Egypt at the young age of thirty, he had to learn many things. Being the manager in the house of Potiphar, an officer of Pharaoh, he learned about the economy and economics. In the jail, where there were many political offenders, he learned many things about running a country and the politics as well as increasing his knowledge and wisdom.

Also, as he met many kinds of people, he learned how to manage human resources, and he also learned about falsehood, betrayal, and the crafty heart of men.

This is one of the programs that God had for Joseph; God wanted to let him rule over a country and embrace the people with love and generosity. That's why the Bible says, even after Joseph was jailed, *"Because the LORD was with him; and whatever he did, the LORD made to prosper"* (Genesis 39:23).

Finally, God began His plan to let Joseph save Egypt from a great calamity. The chief cupbearer and the baker of Pharaoh were condemned and sent to the jail where Joseph was.

One day, each of them had a dream, and as Joseph interpreted each of the dreams, one of them was executed and the other recovered his former position to the Pharaoh.

Two years after that, the Pharaoh had a strange dream. At that time, the chief cupbearer remembered that he was restored to his duty as Joseph interpreted his dream. By his recommendation, Joseph went before the Pharaoh and clearly interpreted the dream that the Pharaoh had dreamt.

The dream that the Pharaoh had was foreshadowing the seven years of great abundance and seven years of famine. Joseph not only interpreted the dream, but he also told them how to prepare for it. That's how Egypt was able to be ready for the famine.

There was little irrigation at the time, so the people had to rely on the rain for agriculture. The seven years of famine meant death. Joseph informed them about a great disaster that could even destroy the whole country. Not only that, but he also gave them the ways and plan to deal with it. How thankful the Pharaoh must have been!

> Then Pharaoh said to his servants, "Can we find a man like this, in whom is a divine spirit?" So Pharaoh said to Joseph, "Since God has informed you of all this, there is no one so discerning and wise as you are. You shall be over my house, and according to your command all my people shall do homage; only in the throne I will be greater than you." Pharaoh said to Joseph, "See, I have set you over all the land of Egypt" (Genesis 41:38-41).

The Pharaoh received great grace from Joseph. He accepted Joseph's family members, namely the Israelites who were also suffering from the famine, into Egypt.

This way, the Israelites could stay in safety and at comfort even during the seven years of famine. They multiplied their numbers in Egypt.

Birth and Trials of Moses

Joseph died and the Pharaoh of the time also died as time passed. A Pharaoh arose in Egypt who did not know about Joseph. Since the Israelites were increasing in numbers, this Pharaoh was afraid and tried to keep them in check.

To stop the Israelites from being multiplied into a large nation, he ordered that all new-born Hebrew boys be put to death. He made the Israelites his slaves and persecuted them. It was a plan to destroy the Israelites as a whole by slowly killing the new born boys.

God promised that Israel would form a great nation but they were rather in the danger of being extinguished. And Moses was born in this gloomy time.

By the order of the Pharaoh, Moses also was supposed to have been killed when he was born, but his mother could not kill him. She hid him for three months for he was a beautiful child. But when she couldn't hide him any more, she put him into wicker basket and put him near the bank of the Nile.

The princess, a daughter of Pharaoh went out there to take a bath. She saw him and took him. Surprisingly, Moses' actual mother, Jochebed, became his nurse, and she was able to teach him about the people of Israel and faith in God from the time he was a young child. All this was done within the plans of God.

God saved him from death and let him learn the best things in the palace of Pharaoh. At the same time God let him be taught about his people and the faith in God from his mother (Acts 7:22).

Moses, being a prince of Egypt, did not take pleasure in the splendid life in the palace, but always had concerns about the people who were suffering. One day, he saw an Egyptian man beating a Hebrew, and in his outrage he killed the Egyptian.

When this was revealed, Moses fled to the land of Midian. The luxurious life as a prince of a strong nation was no more. He had only an arduous life in the wilderness. His plans for his future and the hopes for his people were also gone.

He must have felt so miserable and fearful of his wretched situation. But as the days went by, he forsook the pride and confidence as a prince. He stayed with Jethro, a Midian priest, and became his son-in-law. He now became an ordinary shepherd.

He learned how to shepherd the flock, and he completely humbled himself. In a sense, he became a man of little merit to fulfill God's plans. When he was a prince, he had the confidence and also authority to have been able to do something great for the people of Israel. But now, he was merely a fugitive and a lowly man who couldn't do anything for God.

Likewise, Moses broke down his ego and self-righteousness completely and became an instrument that God could really use.

Men Used by God

The kind of person whom God can use is not a person with his own wisdom and abilities. He is a person who relies on God completely, breaking down his thoughts and denying himself completely to make his obedience complete. It's because we cannot overcome the devil and fulfill God's providence only with men's thoughts and abilities.

Romans 8:7 says, *"Because the mind set on the flesh is hostile toward God; for it does not subject itself to the law of God, for it is not even able to do so and those who are in the flesh cannot please God."* As said, if we have thoughts of flesh, not thoughts of spirit, we cannot obey the word of God.

When King Saul attacked Amalek, God told him to destroy everything there. But Saul captured the king of Amalek and brought back the best animals of the herd and flock. In his opinion it was better and he disobeyed God's word. No matter how good it seems with human thoughts, if it is against the word of God, it already is not a good idea.

Even if we bring good things to offer to God, if it is against the word of God, God cannot accept them. That is why 1 Samuel 15:22 says that obedience is better than sacrifice. King

Saul kept on disobeying the word of God, became arrogant, and finally was forsaken by God. In the very end he had to face a miserable death at the battle of Gilboa.

On the contrary, Peter, who became one of the disciples of Jesus, obeyed the word of Jesus and experienced something really amazing. Peter worked all night but did not catch any fish. Jesus then told him to let down the net into the deep.

Peter said, *"Master, we worked hard all night and caught nothing, but I will do as You say and let down the nets"* (Luke 5:5). When he obeyed, he caught so many fish that his net was almost breaking.

If Peter had said, "Master, I know fishing very well. I am so tired after working all night, and we are wrapping it up. It's very difficult to go to the deep again and let down the net," the work of God would never have happened.

Also, before Jesus went into Jerusalem, He asked two of His disciples to go into the village opposite them and bring a donkey that was tied there and a colt with her (Matthew 21:2-3). The disciples did not use their thoughts but just obeyed, and it was done as Jesus had said.

The important thing about instruments of God is how obedient they are to the word of God until the end. Abraham, Jacob, Joseph, and other fathers of faith obeyed the word of God only with 'Yes' and 'Amen' and that is why God could use them.

God is still looking for men of obedience. He wants the kind of person who forsakes all his theories, knowledge, and his situation and only obeys the will of God completely.

For Moses to obey God and fulfill His providence, he had to humble himself completely staying in the wilderness for forty years. During this time, Moses thoroughly realized that nothing could be done with his own wisdom, ability, or methods.

Looking into this kind of providence of God, we can see that the numbers also have spiritual meanings. Moses fled from Egypt at the age of forty and went through the refining trials for forty years. We can see sufferings have a relationship with the number 'four.'

Also, Israelites had to suffer in Egypt for 400 years, and Moses fasted for forty days to receive the Ten Commandments.

The Calling of Moses

While tending the flock in the wilderness for forty years, Moses learned the patience and meekness necessary to embrace over two million people in the future. That is when God appeared to him. Even while Moses was undergoing the refining trials in the wilderness, the persecutions and the slavery of Israelites in Egypt were still going on.

The sons of Israel sighed because of the bondage, and they cried out; and their cry for help because of their bondage rose up to God. God decided to save the Israelites and appeared before Moses.

One day, Moses was tending the flock on Mount Horeb, and he saw a bush that was burning with fire but not being consumed. He went closer to the bush. At that moment God called Moses.

> *When the LORD saw that he turned aside to look, God called to him from the midst of the bush and said, "Moses, Moses!" (Exodus 3:4)*

When God called him, Moses said, "Here I am." Then God said, *"Do not come near here; remove your sandals from your feet, for the place on which you are standing is holy ground"* (Exodus 3:2-5).

It was an angel of the LORD that appeared as the flames on the bush to show the power of God. The bush certainly had the flames, but it was not consumed by fire. It was to let Moses realize through the power of God that there was a spiritual realm.

God also told Moses to take off his sandals. It's because the most unclean part of body is the feet. In fact, the most unclean part of men is the heart. Men murder, commit adultery, and steal because of the evil in the heart (Matthew 15:18-20). When God told Moses to take off his shoes, it had the intended meaning that God wants men to cast off sins and become sanctified. In other words, God wants the circumcision of heart to sanctify our hearts.

But during the Old Testament times, the circumcision was not done in heart, but in body. That is why God spoke symbolically about taking off the shoes from the feet.

Then, God told Moses to bring the sons of Israel out of Egypt. It was not an easy thing for Moses. He was now just a shepherd, and even if he went back, there was no grounds of support for him.

He was in anguish now. It was sure that Pharaoh wouldn't let the Israelites go. It was unlikely that even his own people would follow him.

> *But Moses said to God, "Who am I, that I should go to Pharaoh, and that I should bring the sons of Israel out of Egypt?" (Exodus 3:11)*

God knew this troubled mind of Moses and He did not just send him. He told him in detail what to tell the people of Israel and the Pharaoh, and that the Pharaoh would not just send the people, and that there would be plagues on Egypt.

God even told him that when the Israelites would go out, they would not go empty-handed but with large quantities of silver and gold, and the clothing of the Egyptians.

God also showed him a piece of evidence. When Moses

followed God's instructions to throw a staff, it turned into a serpent. When he took it by the tail, it turned into a staff again. When he put his hand in his cloak and took it out, his hand was leprous like snow. When he did it again, it was restored like the rest of his flesh.

After hearing the word of God and seeing the signs of God, Moses left for Egypt with the staff, as God had told him. Spiritually, the 'staff' refers to faith. Just like we use it to support our weak legs, we can do anything that is impossible with our own strength, but only if we have faith in the almighty God.

Because Moses knew his shortcomings very well, he was also afraid and somewhat embarrassed, but he relied on faith alone in his way of life-risking venture.

Standards to Distinguish a Man of God

When Moses went to the people of Israel to fulfill God's providence, God proved that he was a man of God not only with words, but with signs that followed his words.

When what he said was realized in reality, and when he did the powerful things that could not be done by men, nobody could deny that God was with him.

Exodus 7:1 says, *"Then the LORD said to Moses, 'See, I make you as God to Pharaoh, and your brother Aaron shall be your prophet.'"* As said, because of the powerful works that were manifested through Moses, he was considered as God by the Pharaoh as well as the people of Israel. Since God made Moses appear like a god, the Pharaoh was too afraid to kill him.

Even now, the Jews pay greatest and utmost respect to Moses as the greatest prophet and teacher. Just as we can see what kind of person Moses was through the power of God manifested through him, we can also distinguish men of God by their fruit.

Deuteronomy 18:22 says, *"When a prophet speaks in the name of the LORD, if the thing does not come about or come true, that is the thing which the LORD has not spoken. The prophet has spoken it presumptuously; you shall not be afraid of him."* We can see whether one is attested by God or not by seeing the fruit of his word.

For example, one who is attested by God serves and loves everybody and is faithful in all God's house, so he is praised by others. Furthermore, he will also perform the powerful works which Moses, the apostle Paul, and Peter performed.

About 3,400 years ago, God sent Moses and saved the sons of Israel from Egypt. And each moment, He sent His men to save His people.

Even in this era where the darkness covers the world, God wants to lead His people through His men who are obedient to Him. He wants to testify to Himself through His power and save countless people from this world that is comparable to Egypt. He wants to take them into the Land of Canaan, which is the heavenly kingdom, the land flowing with milk and honey.

Chapter 2

"I Will Make You as God"

- Ten Plagues -

Exodus 7:1-7

Then the LORD said to Moses, "See, I make you as God to Pharaoh, and your brother Aaron shall be your prophet. You shall speak all that I command you, and your brother Aaron shall speak to Pharaoh that he let the sons of Israel go out of his land. But I will harden Pharaoh's heart that I may multiply My signs and My wonders in the land of Egypt. When Pharaoh does not listen to you, then I will lay My hand on Egypt and bring out My hosts, My people the sons of Israel, from the land of Egypt by great judgments. The Egyptians shall know that I am the LORD, when I stretch out My hand on Egypt and bring out the sons of Israel from their midst." So Moses and Aaron did it; as the LORD commanded them, thus they did. Moses was eighty years old and Aaron eighty-three, when they spoke to Pharaoh.

"Come on! Keep on working!"

Under the whips that the overseers laid on them, the circumstances of slavery for the Israelites were wretched. More than forty years had passed since Moses had fled to the desert of Midian, and the situation in slavery got even worse.

From the midst of the hard labor, the sons of Israel sought the God of whom they had heard from their fathers.

And the sons of Israel sighed because of the bondage, and they cried out; and their cry for help because of their bondage rose up to God (Exodus 2:23).

The 400 years in Egypt had been a long period of time. In the foreign land where there were so many foreign gods, the Israelites' faith in God faded little by little. Their cry was not really from faith in God, but was their earnest plea to God to be set free from the harsh slavery. In a sense they were just hoping for any kind of chance.

Moses Went Before Pharaoh with Faith Alone

The Egyptians made Israel build storage cities Pithom and Raamses, bake bricks, and farm for them. Egyptians were benefiting greatly from the Israelites.

Moses had once been a prince of Egypt, but he was now just a fugitive and a shepherd. There was no chance that the Pharaoh would set the Israelites free just because of the demand of Moses. To the contrary, under such conditions Moses could have been considered a mad man, or he could have been put to death for it.

It was absolutely impossible if he had thought with human thoughts. But God was with him. God Himself attested to Moses' words and promised that he would be able to perform God's power. Moses was worried for he was not a good speaker, and God gave his brother Aaron as the one who would speak for him. God made Moses appear like God to Aaron.

Before Moses arrived in Egypt, God had already appeared to Aaron and told him to go to Mount Horeb and meet with Moses there. When Moses met with his brother Aaron, he told him about every word and sign that God had given him.

Moses arrived in Egypt and called all the elders of Israel. He said, "Elders, God heard your cry and sent me to save you from the hardship."

As the evidence, Moses showed them the staff turning into a serpent and back to the staff, and the hand becoming leprous and recovering. They respectfully bowed their heads low in acknowledgment.

Moses and Aaron boldly went before the Pharaoh with the expectations and ardent desires of their people. They delivered the message that God had told them to let the people of Israel go out from the country into the wilderness and offer sacrifices to God. However, the matter did not go as easily as they had thought.

> *But Pharaoh said, "Who is the LORD that I should obey His voice to let Israel go? I do not know the LORD, and besides, I will not let Israel go" (Exodus 5:2).*

Pharaoh's heart was hardened and he didn't heed God's command. Instead of releasing them, he thought that Israelites were thinking such things because they had much leisure time. Consequently he increased the amount of labor and became harsher on them. The persecution got even more severe.

The foremen pleaded with Pharaoh about this situation, saying, *"Why do you deal this way with your servants? There is no straw given to your servants, yet they keep saying to us, 'Make bricks!'"* (vv. 15-16)

But the reply of Pharaoh was cold.

> *You are lazy, very lazy; therefore you say, "Let us go and sacrifice to the LORD." So go now and work; for you*

will be given no straw, yet you must deliver the quota of bricks (Exodus 5:17-18).

They thought the Pharaoh would free them immediately, but rather they had to face more hardships. Now they came to complain against Moses and Aaron. Even though they were delivering the will of God to them, they didn't want to listen.

Since more than 400 years had passed since they had settled in Egypt, we can understand what kind of faith Israelites had at that time. They had come to hardly know about God any longer.

They just knew that God appeared to their fathers Abraham, Isaac, and Jacob, and He would lead them out of Egypt to the Land of Canaan. In today's sense, they were just like new comers to the church.

Because God knew their level of faith, He did not blame them but began to show His works through Moses. These works were the 'Ten Plagues.'

Ten Plagues Manifested through Moses

God sent Moses and Aaron before the Pharaoh again. To prove that His word was true, God performed a sign.

Just as He allowed Moses to do it at Mount Horeb, when Aaron threw down the staff, it turned into a serpent. But the magicians of Egypt also caused their staffs to become serpents, though they were not as strong as the one made by Aaron. Then, when Pharaoh saw this, he didn't listen to Moses.

In ancient civilizations, sorcerers and magicians often conducted sacrifices. The root of the word 'magic' is in reference to the priests in ancient Persia.

They performed hypnosis, did fortune-telling with the help of evil spirits, and even brought down some kinds of disasters. Pharaoh considered the power of God just to be a matter of these sorceries.

Until the Pharaoh let the Israelites depart from Egypt, one by one God sent Ten Plagues throughout Egypt. These plagues started as a small thing but finally even killed all the first sons of Egypt.

How can these incidents that happened thousands of years ago be related to us today that God let it be written in the Bible in so much detail?

It is to remember that the power of God was manifested throughout all Egypt through His man Moses. But more important reason is the spiritual meaning contained in the Ten Plagues.

God used the situation because He wanted to show us the reasons why people face disasters and the ways to escape from those disasters. The Ten Plagues were not only inflicted upon the Egyptians some thousands of years ago; they represent all kinds of calamities that can take place in our lives today.

Revelation 11:8 says, *"And their dead bodies will lie in the street of the great city which mystically is called Sodom and Egypt, where also their Lord was crucified."* Egypt, in the spiritual sense, refers to this world that is full of sins.

Just as Pharaoh faced so many disasters when he stood against God, those who live in sins will suffer from various problems. All these problems are contained in the 'Ten Plagues'.

The first is the plague of blood. Moses told Aaron to hit the Nile with the staff, and all waters in Egypt turned into blood. How terrible it must have been since all the waters turned into blood! There was the foul smell of blood and dead fish everywhere. Egyptians quickly dug wells to get their drinking water since they couldn't drink or use any water from the river.

> *The fish that were in the Nile died, and the Nile became foul, so that the Egyptians could not drink water from the Nile. And the blood was through all the land of Egypt. So all the Egyptians dug around the Nile for water to drink, for they could not drink of the water of the Nile (Exodus 7:21, 24).*

This plague of blood represents the suffering that comes from the lack of one of the necessities of life. Spiritually, it symbolizes the problems that we face in our surroundings, such as at home or at work.

But when the magicians of Egypt turned water into blood, Pharaoh hardened his heart and didn't listen to Moses. Then, the second plague came.

Countless frogs came up from the Nile and filled the whole nation. But the magicians of Egypt also did the same thing. Not only the streets but also the bedrooms and even kneading bowls were overflowing with frogs.

A bullfrog gets as big as twenty centimeters and its cry is very loud. Though it was not bull frogs that came up to Egypt, just imagine big and repulsive frogs jumping around everywhere. It must have been very disgusting.

A frog is one of the detestable animals, and spiritually, it stands for Satan (Revelation 16:13). The frogs going into the palace, bedrooms, and houses of the Pharaoh's servants and people, symbolizes Satan's inflicting curses on the mankind as a whole, regardless of social position or age. The frogs also went into the ovens and kneading bowls. 'Ovens' refers to workplaces and businesses, and the 'kneading bowl' our daily food.

Therefore, the plague of frogs symbolizes the works of Satan taking place in our homes and workplaces. It is unbearable because Satan is at work at home, at work, and even on the daily food.

The magicians of Egypt made frogs come up, but they couldn't get rid of them. Finally, Pharaoh quickly called Moses and promised him that he would let Israelites go if he removed the frogs. He said:

> *Entreat the LORD that He remove the frogs from me and from my people; and I will let the people go, that they may sacrifice to the LORD (Exodus 8:8).*

Next day, when Moses prayed to God, all the frogs in the palace, houses, and the streets came out and died.

But Exodus 8:15 says, *"But when Pharaoh saw that there was relief, he hardened his heart and did not listen to them, as the LORD had said."* When the Pharaoh was in need, he asked Moses for help but when the situation changed, he changed his mind.

Because God knew this heart of Pharaoh, the plagues continued until he would obey the command of God. Now the third plague came.

Moses told Aaron to raise the staff and hit the dust of the ground, and the dust became gnats. Countless gnats came up onto the people and cattle. The lifeless dust became living gnats, sucking the blood from people and animals, causing itchiness and inflammation.

This plague spiritually symbolizes a situation where small things suddenly come up to the surface and develop into bigger problems, and they cause much pain and suffering. An example would be when some small problems keep mounting between brothers, or between a husband and wife, and later lead to a big fight.

The gnats can live on people when they are not really clean. So, gnats being on men means the plague of gnats happen to those who have latent forms of evil.

The magicians of Egypt could not imitate the plague of gnats nor any of the plagues that followed. They could imitate to some extent changing the water into blood or bringing up frogs from the Nile, but they could not change the dust of the ground into gnats.

Psalm 62:11 says, *"Once God has spoken; twice I have heard this: that power belongs to God."* As said, even with the development of medical science, man can never revive a dead person or create something out of nothing. These works purely belong to God the Creator.

The magicians of Egypt confessed that it was the power of God (Exodus 8:19), but Pharaoh was still stubborn. Even after seeing the power of God, he hardened his heart more and it led to a more serious plague, the plague of flies.

Up to the plague of gnats, if we repent and turn back, we can recover immediately. But from the plague of flies, a wall of sin against God is created, so we would need thorough repentance.

The flies covered not only the houses of people but also the houses of Pharaoh's servants and his palace. It is discomforting and annoying just to see one fly that flies around our food since it carries germs. How painful it would be if we were to see countless flies!

Flies breed in unclean places and diseases are spread wherever they go. Likewise, spiritually, the plague of flies represents a situation where people speak out evil words from their evil heart, and those words are spread here and there. This becomes a snare to them, and they face diseases or problems that are brought upon themselves, their children, their spouses, or workplaces.

> *But the things that proceed out of the mouth come from the heart, and those defile the man. For out of the heart come evil thoughts, murders, adulteries, fornications, thefts, false witness, slanders (Matthew 15:18-19).*

Pharaoh once again asked Moses to remove the flies and then promised he would let the Israelites go, but when the flies actually were removed, he didn't keep his promise.

Finally, the plagues of pestilence and boils were inflicted, and not only the people but also the livestock of Egypt came to suffer. The pestilence is a contagious and infectious disease that is not easy to cure. It is epidemic and spreads inside the body. Many of the livestock in Egypt died because of this pestilence.

The livestock included the horses, the herds, the flocks, goats, and the camels raised by people. They were a major part of the wealth of the king, his servants, and his people. In today's sense, because they are living things, it refers to the family members who are living in one house.

And the pestilence being inflicted upon the livestock means one's evil causes not only himself but his family members to suffer from serious diseases. If a man piles evil upon evil, God has to turn His face away from this person, and the devil will bring many kinds of disasters.

More serious than the pestilence is the plague of boils. Pestilence goes into the body, but the boils are seen on the outside, too. It causes ulcers, itchiness, discharges, and pus. It is a serious case of skin disease or when a certain internal disease worsens and shows on the outside, too.

For example, cancers are in the body only at first, but when it worsens, it may even show on the outside. It's the same with some lung tuberculosis, liver problems, or AIDS. Those who get these diseases are usually short-tempered, arrogant, and have very strong opinions and look down on others, and do not easily accept others' faults.

Other than these cases, one may face the plague of boils when he commits a grave sin in action, or otherwise called works of the flesh, or when his parents, family members, or ancestors have worshiped idols extensively. But even if one's parents worship idols, if the child lives in the word of God, he won't face any calamity because God protects him.

Pharaoh did not turn back even after suffering from those plagues, and the plague of hail with fire came down from heaven. It killed not only the crops all throughout Egypt but also many animals and people who were caught outside.

A large hail-stone may be as big as fifteen centimeters in diameter. That is the size of a large grapefruit. It is unimaginable to think such big hails fall from the sky with fire. It must have caused so much damage not only on the crops but also to the houses and livestock.

Spiritually, the plague of hail refers to unexpected accidents or incidents that cause great damage to one's wealth. It is comparable to when one of the family members is involved in a major accident or has been diagnosed with a serious disease, which resulting costs will be very expensive.

For example, when a believer has desire for money and cares only for earning more money, he may not keep the whole Sabbath. Then, there may be a sudden problem in his workplace or business, and he may even waste his money due to accident or disease. This is like the plague of hail. Because the hail damaged only a part of the crops in the fields, it doesn't mean that everything will be lost as a result of a plague of hail.

But, the crops that remained after the plague of hail were gone completely because of the plague of locusts that followed. The swarm of millions of locusts must have been sheer terror for them.

> *They shall cover the surface of the land, so that no one will be able to see the land. They will also eat the rest of*

what has escaped what is left to you from the hail and they will eat every tree which sprouts for you out of the field. Then your houses shall be filled and the houses of all your servants and the houses of all the Egyptians, something which neither your fathers nor your grandfathers have seen, from the day that they came upon the earth until this day (Exodus 10:5-6).

Once locusts sweep a field, not one blade of grass will remain. It is a terrible calamity. The plague of locusts removes everything, and the damage is much greater than that of the plague of hail.

For example, compared to the plague of hail, the result of the plague of locusts may result in bankruptcy, one's disease would be incurable, or one's child has gone astray to the point of no return. In this case, the whole family or entire business will break down. If we do not repent even after facing this kind of plague, nothing will remain.

Each time a plague came, the Pharaoh promised that he would let the Israelites go, but when the plague was gone, he changed his mind every time.

Now, Moses lifted up his hand toward the sky, and the plague of darkness fell on Egypt. There was no light whatsoever. There was no sun or moon for three days. And how afraid the Egyptians must have been!

> Then the LORD said to Moses, "Stretch out your hand toward the sky, that there may be darkness over the land of Egypt, even a darkness which may be felt." So Moses stretched out his hand toward the sky, and there was thick darkness in all the land of Egypt for three days. They did not see one another, nor did anyone rise from his place for three days (Exodus 10:21-23).

When darkness comes just before the death, it means that darkness covers one's life, and the person has no hope in any aspect of his life. This kind of plague comes upon those who have hardened hearts and will not repent at all, even after they lose everything they have.

It's because they do not acknowledge the existence of God. Even if they confess to believe, they do not keep the word of God but only store up evil. It is a great plague that is close to death, but their life itself is not damaged.

Even after the plague of darkness, Pharaoh did not send the people of Israel out from Egypt. Finally he had to face the plague of the death of the firstborn. Spiritually, it refers to a situation where one's most beloved child or family member dies or goes too deeply into corruption to be saved.

The Ten Plagues became increasingly more serious and more fatal as they were inflicted one by one. Even when the Pharaoh's servants were saying that Egypt was destroyed, the Pharaoh still wouldn't turn from his ways.

As a result God added the plague of the death of all firstborn in Egypt.

> *And all the firstborn in the land of Egypt shall die, from the firstborn of the Pharaoh who sits on his throne, even to the firstborn of the slave girl who is behind the millstones; all the firstborn of the cattle as well (Exodus 11:5).*

God Set the Land of Goshen Apart

Did the Israelites also suffer from the plagues along with the Egyptians?

At that time, the Israelites were staying in Goshen. Because most Israelites were raising cattle which the Egyptians considered detestable, they formed a separate village. But none of the plagues were inflicted upon the land of Goshen.

> *For if you do not let My people go, behold, I will send swarms of flies on you and on your servants and on your people and into your houses; and the houses of the Egyptians will be full of swarms of flies, and also the ground on which they dwell. But on that day I will set apart the land of Goshen, where My people are living, so that no swarms of flies will be there, in order that you may know that I, the LORD, am in the midst of the land (Exodus 8:21-22).*

As recorded, even while the whole land of Egypt was covered with flies, there was not a fly in Goshen. It was the sign that God set the Israelites apart from the Egyptians.

Additionally, they were not affected by the pestilence, boils, hail, and the locusts. The plagues did not come upon the land of Goshen. Even while there was complete darkness all over Egypt, there still was light in Goshen. Those who saw this were amazed and gave glory to God.

Plague of the Death of the Firstborn and Passover

God let the entire land of Egypt know about the death of all the firstborn, and gave instructions to the Israelites. On the day of the great plague on Egypt, they were to take a year old, unblemished, male lamb or goat and put its blood on the lintel and two doorposts. They were also not allowed to go outside until morning.

> *For the LORD will pass through to smite the Egyptians; and when He sees the blood on the lintel and on the two doorposts, the LORD will pass over the door and will not allow the destroyer to come in to your houses to smite you (Exodus 12:23).*

To put the blood on the lintel and the two doorposts symbolizes Jesus Christ and His redeeming blood. It means we can be forgiven of our sins and receive salvation by the blood of the Lord. Concerning this, Jesus said, *"I am the door; if anyone enters through Me, he will be saved, and will go in and out and find pasture"* (John 10:9).

Also, they had to roast the meat and eat it with unleavened bread and bitter herbs. As Jesus said in John 6:53, *"Truly, truly, I say to you, unless you eat the flesh of the Son of Man and drink His blood, you have no life in yourselves,"* we have to take in the flesh of Jesus, namely the word of God.

God also told them not to eat it raw or boiled in water, but to eat its head, legs, and entrails roasted over the fire. It means we have to take in the word of God in the sixty-six books of the Bible by the fire and inspiration of the Holy Spirit.

According to this command of God, the Israelites took an unblemished, one-year-old male lamb or a goat, put its blood on the lintel and doorposts, and ate the meat roasted over the fire.

In the deep night, there was a great cry in Egypt. From the livestock to men, all the firstborn were killed. But the Israelites were safely protected.

> *You shall say, "It is a Passover sacrifice to the LORD who passed over the houses of the sons of Israel in Egypt when He smote the Egyptians, but spared our homes"* (Exodus 12:27).

From this moment up until this day, Israel remembers the grace of God that kept them from the deaths of their firstborn.

They keep the Passover and eat the unleavened bread for seven days remembering the sufferings that they had in Egypt.

Chapter 3

"You Shall Know that I Am the LORD Your God"

- The Exodus -

Exodus 16:11-15

So it came about at evening that the quails came up and covered the camp, and in the morning there was a layer of dew around the camp. When the layer of dew evaporated, behold, on the surface of the wilderness there was a fine flake-like thing, fine as the frost on the ground. When the sons of Israel saw it, they said to one another, "What is it?" For they did not know what it was. And Moses said to them, "It is the bread which the LORD has given you to eat."

Pharaoh did not want to let the Israelites go even while Egypt was afflicted by the various plagues. But, after the plague of the death of the firstborn he finally yielded. All of the firstborn of the Egyptians including the livestock died overnight. The cry of the Egyptians seemed to reach the heavens.

"Oh, my son… son of Pharaoh!"

Pharaoh had hardened his heart, but he had no choice but to give in at the death of his son. He called Moses and told him to take the people of Israel and depart from Egypt.

The Egyptians had to suffer from such great plagues because of the stubbornness of Pharaoh. However, they urged the Israelites to go quickly and gave them silver and gold and even their clothing. Understanding this we can imagine how much they had suffered from the Ten Plagues. God had already told Moses about it when He called him.

> *And it shall be that when you go, you will not go empty-handed. But every woman shall ask of her neighbor and*

the woman who lives in her house, articles of silver and articles of gold, and clothing; and you will put them on your sons and daughters. Thus you will plunder the Egyptians (Exodus 3:21-22).

Everything was done as God had said. Israelites' slavery in Egypt ended, and they now set out for the Promised Land, Canaan.

The Exodus, the Glorious Escape

With Moses at the front, the Israelites left Rameses for Succoth with their flocks and herds. Counting only male adults there were 600,000, so including the children, elderly people, and women there must have been more than two million people. Just imagine this many people moving at one time!

Since they had been raising livestock for 400 years, their flocks and herds were great in number. With the sounds of the animals and the rumblings of wagons, it must have been a commotion.

Children were running around and the elderly persons were also hurrying up not to fall behind the array. They were filled with the joy of being set free and were excited as children on a picnic.

The people could have been just happy with the hope that they would enjoy the blessings in the Canaan Land, but Moses was different. He had to take the responsibility of leading such a great crowd of people all by himself. As Joseph had spoken in his last will requesting to take his corpse to the Promised Land, Moses took the lead with the bones of Joseph.

The shortest way from Egypt to Canaan was to follow the coast line of the Mediterranean, go through the Gaza strip of today, and continue along the route through the land of Philistines.

Because those who were trying to invade Egypt took this route, the border was heavily guarded. Even if they crossed the border, to go to Philistine directly, they would have brought war against them.

But with the faith of Israelites at that time, war was not even an option. They just didn't have enough faith to fight a war. They would have wanted to go back to Egypt instead.

The Israelites were just happy that they were set free from the slavery. They did not have sincere faith in God. If they had any kind of difficulty, they would have wanted to go back to Egypt.

If a big test comes to a new believer and cannot overcome it, he will go back to the world again. Israelites were much the same as this.

Because God knew this situation, He did not take the shortest route but let them cross the Red Sea and wander around in the wilderness, though it was a tougher way to go.

> *Now when Pharaoh had let the people go, God did not lead them by the way of the land of the Philistines, even*

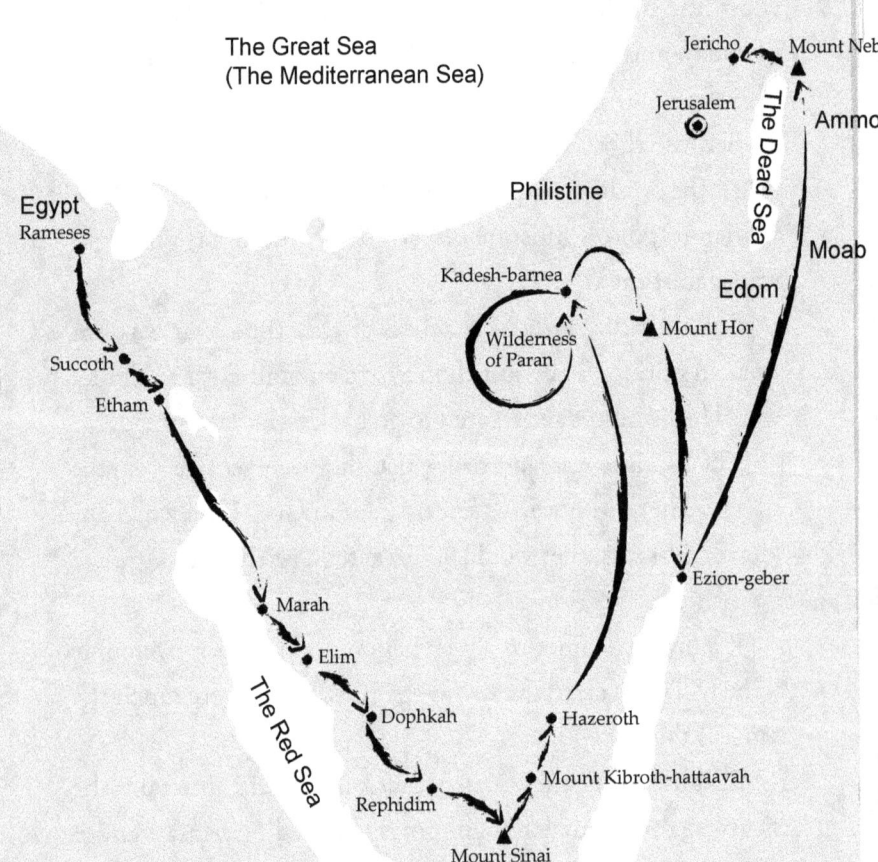

though it was near; for God said, "The people might change their minds when they see war, and return to Egypt" (Exodus 13:17).

The Red Sea Crossing

From the moment the Israelites left Egypt, God moved ahead of them, guiding them with a pillar of clouds by day and a pillar of fire at night. By covering the scorching sunshine in the wilderness with thick clouds, God let them go through the hot wilderness.

In dry parts of the earth, like the deserts of Africa and the Middle East, the temperature is much lower in the shade. Also, God gave them the pillar of fire at night so they could overcome the cold at night in the desert area.

But Israel's peaceful march ended in a short time. They soon found themselves in a dilemma. After Pharaoh let the Israelites go, he regretted it. He took six hundred special war-chariots and all charioteers of Egypt to chase them. God already knew this was going to happen and had already told Moses.

When they had almost reached the Red Sea, the Israelites saw the army of the Pharaoh following them in chariots and horses, raising dust all over. Before them was the Red Sea and from the behind, the Egyptian army was chasing them.

Then, the Israelites complained saying, "We said we would

just serve the Egyptians. Are you killing us in the wilderness because there is no burial place in Egypt? It would have been better for us to serve the Egyptians than to die in the wilderness" (Exodus 14:11). They were crying out to Moses with such great fear.

They came out of Egypt because God heard their cries while they were suffering from slavery. Moses didn't forcefully bring them out. Furthermore, who is God? He allowed fearful plagues in all Egypt and killed all the firstborn of Egypt overnight, but He protected all Israelites.

If they had believed in God who controls life and death, they would not have needed to worry about the Egyptian army at all. But even after seeing such great works of God's power, they still didn't believe in God. Now they were even complaining against God.

But God did not rebuke the Israelites who had such little faith, but He showed a great work of His power through Moses. God did not reprimand the people who had little faith, but He cared for them with the love of a parent who would care for their newborn baby. It was through the faith of Moses that God showed another great work.

Moses spoke boldly to the frightened and trembling Israelites.

> *Do not fear! Stand by and see the salvation of the LORD which He will accomplish for you today; for the*

Egyptians whom you have seen today, you will never see them again forever. The LORD will fight for you while you keep silent (Exodus 14:13-14).

How beautiful a profession of faith this is! Moses did not look at the deep Red Sea or the Egyptian army that was chasing them. He only looked up to the great work of God that He was going to do.

As Moses professed, God began to work for the Israelites. First, the angel of God, who had been going before the camp of Israel, moved and went behind them; and the pillar of cloud moved from before them and stood behind them.

Then, during the night, the side of the Israelites had light, but there was only cloud and darkness on Egyptian side. They Egyptian army could not march forward in the complete darkness.

Finally, Moses stretched out his staff as God commanded him. By a strong east wind that blew all night the LORD swept the sea back and turned the sea into dry land, so the waters were divided.

Just imagine this magnificent scene in your mind.

With the sound of thunder and a great wind, the vast sea was divided, and the people were walking in the middle of the sea. The waters formed walls on either side.

Just imagine yourself walking in the middle of this sea. You must be trembling with awe and astonished at the great work of God's power. Wouldn't you give glory to God for showing you such a wonderful work and praise and worship Him from the depth of heart?

More than two million people including children and elderly people and their flocks and herds were crossing through the middle of the sea.

But the Egyptian army, which could not move in the darkness, soon caught up with and followed them. They also entered into the way that was made in the sea. It seemed they would catch up with the Israelites very soon, but they had great difficulty chasing them.

The chariot wheels were coming off and they had great difficulty driving the chariots. Some of those soldiers who felt something strange thought, "Let us flee from Israel, for the LORD is fighting for them against the Egyptians."

Their feeling was right. When the Israelites finished crossing the divided Red Sea, Moses stretched out his hand over the sea again. Then the parted Red Sea returned to its normal state.

"Oh-oh!"

In an instant, the whole Egyptian army was buried in the water.

At this moment, Moses and the Israelites praised and

worshiped God with their thanks to God for saving them from the hands of the Egyptians. Moses' feeling was much different from others since he was responsible for the safety of the people.

> The LORD is my strength and song, and He has become my salvation; this is my God, and I will praise Him; my father's God, and I will extol Him (Exodus 15:2).

> Who is like You among the gods, O LORD? Who is like You, majestic in holiness, awesome in praises, working wonders? (Exodus 15:11)

Moses' sister Miriam and the women also danced with timbrel in their hands, giving glory to God.

> Sing to the LORD, for He is highly exalted; the horse and his rider He has hurled into the sea (Exodus 15:21).

The Ten Plagues was amazement itself, but God confirmed once again that He was with the Israelites. He confirmed and attested Moses by parting the Red Sea.

Because Moses had the faith to obey even the things that could not really be obeyed, they could see the wondrous work of God.

God's command to part the sea could not have been obeyed if Moses had held to any human thoughts or theories.

But when he obeyed with faith, the sea was parted by God's power. All of these things that belong to God are possible only by faith.

Israelites' Complaining at Marah

After they crossed the Red Sea, the Israelites went into the wilderness of Shur. Without being able to get any drinking water, they arrived at a place called 'Marah.' They finally found the water, but the water there was too bitter to drink.

They soon began to complain against Moses again.

They witnessed the Ten Plagues, and they crossed Red Sea on dry land just three days ago, but they immediately and without hesitation began to pour out their complaints as soon as they had difficulty in reality.

Of course, it must have been difficult for them when they were not able to get any drinking water for three days in the dry heat of the wilderness. But still they were not able to have even minimal faith thinking, "The almighty God who divided the Red Sea will give us water if we ask."

But the patient God showed Moses a tree and had him throw it into the waters to change the bitter water into sweet water. Here, what is the reason that God made Moses throw a tree into the water?

It shows us that with God's work, He can make water sweet even through a tree. Namely, it shows us that God is almighty, that He can create things from nothing and make the impossible possible. Also, it was to let the Israelites understand that they were no different from dry tree branches for they kept on complaining in every difficult matter, even though they had experienced amazing works of God.

Water refers to living water, which is the word of God. And when a dry tree was thrown into the water, the water soon turned sweet. It means even a person who is thrown out like a dry tree can be renewed if he lives by the word of God.

Once Again Repeatedly Complaining

Then they set out from Elim, and all the congregation of the sons of Israel came to the wilderness of Sin, which is between Elim and Sinai. But they had another problem. The food that they brought with them from Egypt had run out.

They remembered the times when they had enough bread to eat in Egypt, and they soon began to complain. They already forgot the memory of harsh slavery and persecution.

The Israelites couldn't tolerate anything. They immediately complained whenever they faced something difficult. But God still did not hold them in account for it. Instead, He fed them with manna and quail. It was because, when they followed Moses and did not break away from the mass of the Exodus in the wilderness, God deemed it as faith.

Every evening quail came and covered their camp. In the

morning, there was a layer of dew around the camp. When the layer of dew evaporated, on the ground in the wilderness there was a fine flake-like substance, almost as fine as frost, covered the ground. It was 'manna' that came down from heaven. It was white, and its taste was like wafers with honey.

God told them to take only as much as they needed (Exodus 16:16) and not leave any that they had gathered until morning. But when some of the people disobeyed and left some of it until morning it became worm-ridden and foul.

With the manna and quail that God gave to them, they could march on with enough food, even in the barren wilderness.

As time passed, rather than the hope for the Canaan Land that flows with milk and honey, the Israelites felt increasingly aggravated because of the barrenness of the life in the wilderness. The only thing that they could see was the wilderness and mountains of rocks.

They set out from the wilderness of Sin, according to the command of the LORD, and camped at Rephidim, and there was no water for the people to drink. Therefore the people quarreled with Moses and said, "Give us water that we may drink."

Some of them were so ill-tempered toward Moses that they were about to stone him. What would Moses have felt in his heart at this point?

So Moses cried out to the LORD, saying, "What shall I do to this people?" (Exodus 17:4)

Moses could only pray to God. Then the LORD said to Moses, *"Pass before the people and take with you some of the elders of Israel; and take in your hand your staff with which you struck the Nile, and go"* (v. 5). God told him to strike the rock at Horeb. When Moses did in front of the elders of Israel what God had told him, water came out of the rock.

Even after that the people of Israel still could not show faith when they faced various difficulties. The sympathetic concern that Moses had each time cannot be expressed with words.

He had to pray on behalf of the people who did not have the faith to pray and bring down God's grace for themselves. At the same time, he had to calm them down, teach them the truth, and plant faith in them.

While they were grumbling and complaining at Rephidim, the Amalekite forces attacked them. Moses told Joshua to choose men for their close combat skill and go out, and fight against Amalek. Then he stationed himself on the top of the hill with the staff of God in his hand to pray. At this time when Moses' two hands were raised, the Israelites were winning, but when his hands were lowered the Amalekite forces would win.

As time passed and Moses' arms were tired, Aaron and

Hur took a stone and put it under him, and he sat on it; and they supported his hands, one on one side and one on the other. Thus his hands were steady until the sun set. It was in this way that they were able to win the battle.

Ten Commandments and the Statutes and the Law

Now Jethro, the priest of Midian, Moses' father-in-law, took Moses' wife Zipporah, and her two sons and went to Moses. Moses told him in detail the amazing works of God that had taken place during the Exodus. Jethro praised and worshipped God and they rejoiced together.

Next day, Jethro saw something strange. Many people had lined up to see Moses and to ask the will of God. As one person finished speaking to Moses, another person began to explain his situations to him. The line never got shorter, and even the whole day was not enough.

Before, when the Israelites lived in Egypt, they were under the control of the laws of Egypt. But from the time they departed Egypt there was no law for them. So, they came to Moses for mediation in trials and judgments. Can you imagine what it would have been like since Moses was but one person and he was dealing with more than two million people!

Jethro advised Moses to select from among all the people those able men who feared God, men of truth, and men who hated dishonest gain. He further advised that Moses should place these men over the people as leaders of thousands, of hundreds, of fifties and of tens for minor disputes, and that Moses was to deal with only major disputes. Jethro asked Moses to do so if God allowed him to do it (Exodus 18:23). Though he was a Gentile, he knew the principle very well.

Moses thought it was good and appointed leaders of thousands, hundreds, fifties and tens. But he still had to give them the law which could be the standard and rule for judgment. So, God guided them to the Mount Sinai and let them sanctify themselves. Then He gave them the Ten Commandments and the Law through Moses.

The Israelites were afraid of the appearance of God the LORD at Mount Sinai. On behalf of them, God called Moses to Sinai. There, God Himself engraved the Ten Commandments on the stone tablets and gave him the Law.

> *I am the LORD your God, who brought you out of the land of Egypt, out of the house of slavery. (v.2)*
> *You shall have no other gods before Me ... (v. 3)*
> *You shall not make for yourself an idol ... You shall not worship them or serve them ... (vv. 4-5)*
> *You shall not take the name of the LORD your God in vain ... (v.7)*
> *Remember the Sabbath day, to keep it holy ... (v.8)*
> *Honor your father and your mother ... (v.12)*
> *You shall not murder ... (v.13)*
> *You shall not commit adultery ... (v.14)*

You shall not steal ... (v.15)
You shall not bear false witness against your neighbor ... (v.16)
You shall not covet your neighbor's house ... (v.17)
(Exodus 20:2-17)

Furthermore, God gave them the detailed statutes and laws concerning the altar, servants, violence, restitution, morality, justice, and welfare.

The Ten Commandments can be considered as comparable to the constitution of a country today. The statutes and laws are the rules and regulations governing civil, criminal, and family cases. The statutes and laws were detailed ordinances and regulations of the Ten Commandments. They dealt with the problems that could rise in their everyday life.

They were the ordinances given according to the social structure at that time, with God's justice and love. Therefore, the Ten Commandments and the ordinances were not given to lay a burden on the Israelites.

Especially, the Ten Commandments are not just some rules. They were the absolute command going beyond the level of personal morality. The Ten Commandments may seem to be the law and ordinances on the outside, but it also contains the covenant of salvation.

The Israelites were spared from the deaths of firstborn in Egypt by putting the blood, which represents the blood of the Lord Jesus, on the sides and lintel of the door. Likewise, they could receive salvation when they lived in the word of God by keeping the Ten Commandments.

Furthermore, God did not just give His own commandments and forced them to obey them. He first let the Israelites experience many powerful works so that they could believe and willingly obey. The Ten Commandments was a strict standard by which the Israelites could become God's chosen people or not.

Likewise, even today, keeping the commandments of God will affect our salvation and it will also decide whether we can receive the love and blessings of God.

The Ten Commandments are the consolidation of all sixty-six books of the Bible, the word of God. If we understand the spiritual meaning in them and keep them then we will be able to understand the will of God and follow it.

The Tabernacle

On the Mount Sinai, God also told Moses about the tabernacle in detail. The tabernacle was a place for God to dwell; in a sense it is like a church today.

The tabernacle as a whole was a holy place. Especially the room of the Holy of Holies was set apart within the tabernacle. Only the high priest could enter there once a year for the atonement of sins, and sinners could not go in there.

But when Jesus died on the cross for us, the curtain that

separated the Holy of Holies was torn into two. It means that the way for us to go before God was opened (Hebrews 10:19-20). Before this time the people could go to God only through the priests, but now we can communicate with God directly.

The reason why God let them build the tabernacle was because He knew the heart of men very well. Because He knew the desires of men who wanted to see things that are visible and touch things that are tangible, God let them build the visible tabernacle and let His glory remain above it.

Furthermore, it was also for the forgiveness of sins. It's because, after the Ten Commandments and the statutes and laws were given, it was inevitable that people would commit crimes.

The law of the Old Testament is 'an eye for an eye, a tooth for a tooth, a hand for a hand, and a foot for a foot.' Since it was not the era of the Holy Spirit, they were not able to discover the sins and evil in their hearts. So, the only way to prevent crimes was strict retribution. Just as a little bit of yeast will spread through the loaf very quickly, even a small crime could spread and develop very quickly if it was left untreated. That's why God gave them strict punishment.

But suppose a person accidentally caused the hand of another person to become disabled, and he had to cause his hand to be disabled according to the Law. Then many of the Israelites would have been disabled before they reached the Canaan Land.

Therefore, God opened a way for those who committed sins

to come to the tabernacle with their sacrifices, so that they could be forgiven of their sins. The book of Leviticus writes about different ways of sacrifices and ways of atonement through which sinners could be forgiven of their sins before God.

As said, *"You shall be holy, for I am holy"* (Leviticus 11:45), the book of Leviticus is the guide book for reconciliation between God and men. It focuses on how sins can be forgiven, and how people can lead a holy life like the Holy God. Also, the sacrifices that were made through the arbitration of priests symbolizes that we can go to God only through Jesus Christ.

The Love of Moses, a Man of God

Moses was fasting for forty days on the Mount Sinai while receiving the Ten Commandments and the details about the tabernacle. Sinai is a mountain of rocks where it is difficult even for a tree to grow to provide cover from the scorching sun.

While Moses was fasting and communicating with God in this desolate place, where he couldn't even get drinking water, something completely unexpected was going on in the camp of the people.

Since there was no news from Moses, who was on the Mount, the people became impatient and requested something of Aaron.

> *Make a god for us who will go before us; for this Moses, the man who brought us up from the land of Egypt, we do*

not know what has become of him (Exodus 32:23).

Aaron could not put up with the requests of the people any longer and he made a golden calf. Israel committed the grave sin of idolatry. They were giving sacrifices before the image of the calf and enjoyed themselves eating and drinking. They had received so much grace from God, but they forsook God.

To receive the will of God and guide the people, Moses was fasting without even drinking water for forty days, but the people were worshiping an idol, which God abhors. What would Moses have felt when he saw them committing such a sin?

Moses' heart was so inflamed by what they had done that he threw the tablets from his hands and shattered them at the foot of the mountain. He took the calf and ground it to powder, and made the sons of Israel drink it. God was so angry with them that He said He was about to destroy them. God told Moses that He would raise up a nation through him.

We can find people in world history who planned treachery to drive away the king and take the throne. They did it for their own interests or advantage. Those who have such desire would love to form a country through themselves and give the nation to his descendants.

And God was saying that He would form a great nation through one person. That person was Moses. But Moses rather offered up his own life to save the people of Israel who were acting with such evil.

> *Alas, this people has committed a great sin, and they have made a god of gold for themselves. But now, if You will, forgive their sin—and if not, please blot me out from Your book which You have written! (Exodus 32:31-32)*

Here, 'Your book which You have written' is the Book of Life in which the names of those who are saved are recorded. Those whose names are not written in this book will fall into eternal fire of hell.

Moses knew exactly what it meant to be blotted out from the Book of Life, and he knew better than anybody about the fear of hell. But he was pleading with God for the people offering his own spirit. Through his desperate prayer, God forgave the people once again.

From the book of Psalms we can understand how the sons of Israel broke Moses' heart.

> *How often they rebelled against Him in the wilderness and grieved Him in the desert! (Psalm 78:40)*

This is the same thing that is happening today. There are people who are healed of diseases that cannot be cured by medical science or who have received answers to various problems of life. But after time passes, they think it was coincidence, and they doubt and leave God. This is what grieves God so much.

The Covenant Re-established and the Tabernacle Completed

When the incident was settled by the compassion of God, Moses cut out two stone tablets like the former ones and went to the Mount Sinai again. He fasted another forty days and received the Ten Commandments on the tablets.

Then, he came back to the people, called the congregation and told them to willingly give offerings for the tabernacle of the LORD God.

> *Take from among you a contribution to the LORD; whoever is of a willing heart, let him bring it as the LORD's contribution: gold, silver, and bronze (Exodus 35:5).*

The people immediately went to their tents to bring the offerings to God. Some brought their earrings and signet rings and bracelets, all articles of gold. Some others brought goats' skins and rams' skins and pure unblemished leather. Skilled women spun goat thread with their hands, and brought what they had spun.

> *Everyone whose heart stirred him and everyone whose spirit moved him came and brought the LORD's contribution for the work of the tent of meeting and for all its service and for the holy garments (Exodus 35:21).*

Everyone presented his offerings with cheerful mind. They brought much more than enough for the construction work. Moses had to tell them to stop bringing any more offerings. God is always delighted with offerings that are given with willingness and cheerful heart.

Some people criticize churches that build big church buildings saying it is better to do charitable works with that money. But it is very important to construct the sanctuary of God with the strength of not only a couple of persons but the entire congregation.

Finally, the sons of Israel began to construct the tabernacle which God commanded them to build. First, they set up the tabernacle. Then they made the ark of testimony (also called the ark of the covenant), the table, lampstand, the altar of incense, altar of burnt offering, and the robes of the priests.

Now they finished the construction of the tabernacle and it was time to offer it to God. Moses put the ark of the testimony into the tabernacle, put the table, and arranged what belonged on it, lit the lamps on their lampstands. He let Aaron and his sons wash them with water and put holy garments on them.

At this time, clouds had settled on the tabernacle and the glory of God filled it. Since then, the cloud of God was over the tabernacle during the day, and the fire was in the clouds at night. The whole congregation could feel God was with them.

Whenever the cloud was taken up from over the tabernacle, the sons of Israel would set out; but if the cloud was not taken up, then they did not set out (Exodus 40:36-38).

Of course, God guided them with the pillars of fire and cloud from Egypt until that time. But after the dedication of the tabernacle, the cloud remained over the tabernacle, so the Israelites could feel the presence of God more clearly.

The same kind of thing was symbolically constructed in the Temple that Solomon built. There were two pillars called Jachin and Boaz, and they symbolized the pillars of fire and cloud through which God guided them in the wilderness.

Sin of Standing against a Man of God

Even though they received the commandment of God and made the tabernacle, it doesn't mean the Israelites changed completely. When faced with difficulties, they complained against Moses, and when they didn't agree with something, they even criticized him saying he was unrighteous.

For example, when Moses took an Ethiopian woman for his wife, his brother Aaron and his sister Miriam criticized him. Numbers 12:2 says, *"Has the LORD indeed spoken only through Moses? Has He not spoken through us as well?"* They meant they had the authority to rebuke a wrongdoing of Moses because they were also prophets of God.

If, as Miriam and Aaron said, it had been true that Moses violated the word of God and they were more righteous than

Moses, God would have chosen them, not Moses.

But God chose Moses. Furthermore, God did not forgive Miriam and Aaron for criticizing Moses, for he was faithful in all God's household and was a man after God's heart.

> *[The LORD] said, "Hear now My words: If there is a prophet among you, I, the LORD, shall make Myself known to him in a vision I shall speak with him in a dream. Not so, with My servant Moses, he is faithful in all My household; with him I speak mouth to mouth, even openly, and not in dark sayings, and he beholds the form of the LORD. Why then were you not afraid to speak against My servant, against Moses?" (Numbers 12:6-8)*

God poured His wrath on Miriam and Aaron who criticized Moses, and Miriam became leprous. Moses prayed to God to heal her, but God healed her only after she stayed outside of the camp for seven days. Likewise, to criticize a man of God is not a little sin.

But today, there are many people who within their personal opinions judge and criticize churches or those who follow the will of God. For example, if a church becomes big, enlarging the kingdom of God, some people say it is "commercialism." They also say slanderous words about those who perform powerful works of God and preach the gospel.

Also, there are even some people who make false rumors

to criticize churches. This can easily be a grave sin, for it is to hinder the kingdom of God.

While they were marching towards the Canaan Land, the Israelites saw many signs and wonders, but they continuously contested and complained against God and Moses, the man of God. However, God was patient with them; He just showed them so many powerful works so that their faith could grow. He worked through the faith of one person, Moses.

Also, whenever He performed a great work, He said, *"You shall know that I am the LORD your God"* (Exodus 16:12). God earnestly wanted them to grow in faith through seeing the power of God. God guided them to know and believe in God by experiencing the works of the almighty God and to obey with their heart.

Here, to know God is not just to know Him in knowledge. 1 John 2:4 says, *"The one who says, 'I have come to know Him,' and does not keep His commandments, is a liar, and the truth is not in him."* To know God is to cast off all sins and evil and resemble God who is light.

Therefore, the time in the wilderness was very necessary for the sons of Israel. They witnessed so many powerful works of God through their leader Moses and were guided by God. They finally reached Kadesh-barnea. Before their eyes was the Canaan Land, the land where they had longed so much to enter.

Chapter 4

"If the LORD Is Pleased with Us"

- Confession of Joshua and Caleb -

Numbers 14:6-9

Joshua the son of Nun and Caleb the son of Jephunneh, of those who had spied out the land, tore their clothes; and they spoke to all the congregation of the sons of Israel, saying, "The land which we passed through to spy out is an exceedingly good land. If the LORD is pleased with us, then He will bring us into this land and give it to us a land which flows with milk and honey. Only do not rebel against the LORD; and do not fear the people of the land, for they will be our prey. Their protection has been removed from them, and the LORD is with us; do not fear them."

The Israelites reached the entrance of the Promised Land of Canaan one year after the Exodus from Egypt. Normally, from Egypt to Canaan, it would have taken only several days if they had taken the shortcut. Even with many people, it would have taken only a couple of months.

But God guided them to a safer way, into the wilderness, though they had to go around. It was to avoid conflict with another people called the Philistines.

Just imagine more than two million people, along with their cattle, needing to pass through the land of another country. What country would just stand by and watch? Even though the Israelites didn't intend to invade them, with such a disruption and inconvenience to the Philistines, a conflict was something that could be expected.

In their march through the wilderness, they sometimes stayed at one place for days or even for months. As said in Numbers 9:22, *"Whether it was two days or a month or a year that the cloud lingered over the tabernacle, staying above it, the sons of Israel remained camped and did not set out; but when it was lifted, they did set out,"* without the cloud leading them, they did not set out.

Whenever they faced difficult situations, to give them the opportunities to gain faith, God let them see His power through Moses. It was because the faith of the whole congregation of Israel was necessary for them to go into Canaan. They came out of Egypt through the faith in the work of God by one person, Moses. But to win the battles against the peoples in Canaan and conquer the land, the faith of Israel as a whole had to increase.

Twelve Spies at Kadesh-Barnea

Finally, the Israelites arrived at Kadesh-Barnea, just below the Land of Canaan. God had Moses select one leader from each of the twelve tribes to scout the land for forty days.

Because there were other people living there, they had to get some information about those people and the land before they could fight against them. This was the beginning of the test to go into the Land of Canaan.

In order for us to receive God's blessings, we first have to prepare the vessel to receive them. Of course, it is by God's grace that we receive blessings. But, as our faith grows we must first have the qualifications to receive the blessings.

For example, the father of faith, Abraham, became a person who was right in God's heart through trials. But God did not just bless him. Only when he proved his faith by passing the test of giving his only son, Isaac, did God give him the blessing to become the 'source of blessings.'

The twelve leaders from each tribe had to show their faith after they scouted the Land of Canaan. Just before entering into the land, the people of Israel must have had great expectations for these men. They probably hoped that these men would become their eyes, ears and hearts in seeing the land.

Moses also gave them some advice to follow in scouting the land before they went.

> *Go up there into the Negev; then go up into the hill country. See what the land is like, and whether the people who live in it are strong or weak, whether they are few or many. How is the land in which they live, is it good or bad? And how are the cities in which they live, are they like open camps or with fortifications? How is the land, is it fat or lean? Are there trees in it or not? Make an effort then to get some of the fruit of the land (Numbers 13:17-20).*

They scouted the Land of Canaan for forty days, and surely as God said, it was a land flowing with milk and honey. The soil was good and the fruits and crops were abundant.

When they reached the valley of Eschol, located at southwestern part of Jerusalem, they saw very good grapes. As

Moses commanded them to bring some of the fruit, they cut a single cluster of grapes. It was so big that they had to carry it on a pole between two men. They also took some of the pomegranates and figs.

But the problem was the people there. There were several different peoples in the Canaan Land. They were very big and very strong. They were the sons of Anak, the part of the Nephilim.

Nephilim in Hebrew means 'huge person.' They were so big that these spies thought they were like locusts compared to those people. Goliath of the Philistines was six cubits and a span tall, which was close to three meters. So now we have an idea just how big the Canaanites were.

As they were big, their cities and the fortifications were also big (Deuteronomy 1:28). Ten of the twelve spies were disheartened when they saw the reality of the situation.

Different Confessions of Twelve Spies

The Israelites heard the reports from the leaders who came back from scouting the land, and they were disturbed. At that time, one of the twelve spies, Caleb the son of Jephunne, tried to calm the people down and boldly said, "Let's go up and take the land. We are more than able to overcome them!" But what he heard was harsh criticism from the other spies who scouted the land.

> *"We are not able to go up against the people, for they are too strong for us." So they gave out to the sons of Israel a bad report of the land which they had spied out, saying, "The land through which we have gone, in spying it out, is a land that devours its inhabitants; and all the people whom we saw in it are men of great size. There also we saw the Nephilim (the sons of Anak were part of the Nephilim); and we became like grasshoppers in our own sight, and so we were in their sight" (Numbers 13:31-33).*

The Israelites believed the negative and disheartening reports from the other ten spies rather than the words of Caleb.

"We came here all the way from Egypt, and if we cannot go into the Canaan Land, what should we do in this wilderness where it's difficult to find one plant?"

In deep despair, they began to complain against Moses and Aaron, and against God.

> *All the sons of Israel grumbled against Moses and Aaron; and the whole congregation said to them, "Would that we had died in the land of Egypt! Or would that we had died in this wilderness! Why is the LORD bringing us into this land, to fall by the sword? Our wives and our little ones will become plunder; would it not be better for us to return to Egypt?" (Numbers 14:2-3)*

The Israelites cried and lamented all night and they finally came up with a plan to appoint another leader and return to Egypt. However there were two whose hearts were burning over this tense situation.

Among the twelve spies, only Joshua and Caleb had mourning hearts seeing the people who didn't have faith, and they began to plead with them while rending their clothes.

> *The land which we passed through to spy out is an exceedingly good land. If the LORD is pleased with us, then He will bring us into this land and give it to us a land which flows with milk and honey. Only do not rebel against the LORD; and do not fear the people of the land, for they will be our prey. Their protection has been removed from them, and the LORD is with us; do not fear them (Numbers 14:7-9).*

But even their truthful confessions of faith were useless against the people who were already disheartened. The people were even going to stone the two men. They couldn't deal with the reality of such a difficult situation.

But men of faith do not look at the reality of things. They just understand what God's will is and know that they can do anything if God is with them. Then they act on their confessions to produce deeds of faith.

Psalm 37:4 says, *"Delight yourself in the LORD; and He will give you the desires of your heart."* Hebrews 11:6 says, *"And without faith it is impossible to please Him, for he who comes to God must believe that He is and that He is a rewarder of those who seek Him."*

If we please God with confessions and deeds of faith, the impossible will become possible by God's power. But even after experiencing so many works of God, except for Joshua and Caleb, the Israelites failed in the test of faith to please God.

The Israelites Rejected God

God was angry with the Israelites who kept on complaining. God said that He would destroy them with pestilence.

> *The LORD said to Moses, "How long will this people spurn Me? And how long will they not believe in Me, despite all the signs which I have performed in their midst? I will smite them with pestilence and dispossess them, and I will make you into a nation greater and mightier than they" (Numbers 14:11-12).*

> *Pardon, I pray, the iniquity of this people according to the greatness of Your lovingkindness, just as You also have forgiven this people, from Egypt even until now (Numbers 14:19).*

The hope for the Canaan Land was now gone like bubbles. Their lives could be spared only by the intercession of Moses, and except for Joshua and Caleb, who had made positive confessions of faith, nobody in the first generation of the Exodus was able to enter into the Land of Canaan.

As they had confessed saying, "Would that we had died in the land of Egypt! Or would that we had died in this wilderness!" they died in the wilderness. Then, the promise of God concerning the Canaan Land was passed down to their children who were younger than twenty, but they still had to wander around in the wilderness for forty years because of their parents' sin.

It was the forty days of spying out the land by the spies that turned into forty years, and the ten spies who brought out the very bad reports of the land and made all the congregation grumble died by a plague before the LORD (Numbers 14:36-38).

Therefore, we should understand how important confessions from our lips are, and nothing should be spoken recklessly. We have to be honest and precise in our words, and it is important to make positive confessions of faith and not to speak negative words.

God set the sons of Israel free from Egypt through the Ten Plagues. He let them cross the Red Sea like it was dry land. He changed bitter water into sweet water; gave them manna and quail; and gave them water from a rock. He guided them with a pillar of cloud by day and fire by night until they stood before the Land of Canaan. Still, their stubbornness and lack of faith was no different from when they were in Egypt.

The Beginning of Life in the Wilderness

The Israelites began to regret and lament after hearing the word of God through Moses and seeing the ten spies die by plague.

> *In the morning, however, they rose up early and went up to the ridge of the hill country, saying, "Here we are; we have indeed sinned, but we will go up to the place which the LORD has promised" (Numbers 14:40).*

They say they will attack the Canaan Land now, but it was too late. Moses knew very well that God was not with them since they sinned, and he tried to stop them.

> *Do not go up, or you will be struck down before your enemies, for the LORD is not among you. For the Amalekites and the Canaanites will be there in front of you, and you will fall by the sword, inasmuch as you have turned back from following the LORD. And the LORD will not be with you (Numbers 14:42-43).*

Despite Moses' advice, some people still went and attacked the hill country. The result was a terrible defeat. Going into Canaan Land like that was neither obedience nor faith.

A similar example would be a student failing a college entrance exam but came to know the answers to the test he took. But it doesn't mean he can now be accepted to the college. Something like this should not happen. He has to study one more year, take the exam again and prove himself.

In the same way, when some Israelites went up to the hill country, it doesn't mean they now had faith; they were just pretending to have faith. Rather than going into Canaan Land like that, they had to repent of their evilness thoroughly and make up their minds to have spiritual faith.

If they had really repented from the depth of their heart, the situation could have been different. But this action of theirs was not done with an attitude of repentance. They just wanted to avoid punishment and tried to cover their fault. And, once again it resulted in disobedience. Because of this, they had to face the pain of complete defeat, and finally, they began the forty-year life of wandering in the wilderness.

Do you feel Israelites acted foolishly? The fact is that many people today are not much different from Israelites at that time.

When we were going the way of death, God sent His one and only Son to us. He redeemed us from sins and guided us to the way of salvation. But even believers forget that grace and complain against God when they face difficulties.

The first generation of the Exodus did not repent and turn back even after receiving the punishment of wandering around in the wilderness. They did not cast off evil from their hearts and they had no faith. This evil heart of Israel led them to another big incident that caused great disaster to come upon the whole congregation of Israel; it was the rebellion of Korah.

The Rebellion of Korah

The Israelites went into the wilderness by the word of God. They hated their life in the wilderness so much that one of the Levites named Korah tempted the people to stand against Moses.

Korah was a cousin of Moses. He thought Moses was no better than he was in any way. He didn't like the fact that Moses and Aaron had the authority of a priest. He tempted 250 influential leaders to join him and stood against Moses with them.

> *They assembled together against Moses and Aaron, and said to them, "You have gone far enough, for all the congregation are holy, every one of them, and the LORD is in their midst; so why do you exalt yourselves above the assembly of the LORD?" (Numbers 16:3)*

He was actually asking who Moses and Aaron thought they were and how they had been appointed as leaders. Especially, Dathan and Abiram spoke in complete nonsense saying something like, "Is it not bad enough that you have brought us up out of a land flowing with milk and honey to have us die in the wilderness, and now you would also lord it over us!"

When Moses fell on his face before God, God told him and Aaron to separate themselves from among the congregation, that He would consume them instantly (Numbers 16:21). But Moses asked for forgiveness saying, *"O God, God of the spirits of all flesh, when one man sins, will You be angry with the entire congregation?"* (v. 22) God gave him an answer.

As Moses finished speaking about the death of Korah, Dathan, and Abiram, the ground that was under them and their families split open. Korah and his family and all men who belonged to him with all their possessions fell into the earth. And then the earth closed over them.

Fire also came forth from the LORD and consumed the two hundred and fifty men who were offering the incense. By now the people should have realized what God's will was. But instead they complained against Moses and Aaron saying that they caused the deaths of the people of the LORD.

When they faced the punishment of wandering around the wilderness, if they truly regretted their evilness and repented, they would not have stood with Korah. They would not have stood with a man who stood against the man of God, Moses.

But because they did not cast off evil from the heart and stood against God, a plague began and 14,700 people died.

The Budding of Aaron's Rod and Bronze Serpent

The patient God planned something to let the people understand once again.

God told Moses to get a rod from the leaders of each tribe, a total of twelve rods. God had him write the name of the leaders of each tribe on the rods, and then He had the rods be put in the tent of testimony. God wanted to show them evidence by making the rod of the chosen one bud overnight.

A rod is a dead tree that has been trimmed, so how can it bud? But by the work of God, one of the dry rods budded overnight. Not only that, it had produced blossoms, and it bore ripe almonds.

The rod obviously belonged to Aaron, the speaker and prophet for Moses. God directly showed the people that He was with Moses and Aaron. He showed them such evidence to let them have faith.

But even this sign was useless for them. Even after they had seen this, when they had no drinking water or became tired of eating manna every day, they complained in the same way as before.

The people thus contended with Moses and spoke, saying, "If only we had perished when our brothers perished before the LORD! Why then have you brought the LORD's assembly into this wilderness, for us and our beasts to die here? Why have you made us come up from Egypt, to bring us in to this wretched place? It is not a place of grain or figs or vines or pomegranates, nor is there water to drink" (Numbers 20:3-5).

They even called manna given by God 'worthless bread,' thus despising the grace of God (Numbers 21:5). So, the punishment of God was inflicted upon them; fiery serpents with poison came out and bit many people and killed them. Only then did the people repent.

When Moses prayed for the people, God gave him a way to avoid the disaster. God had him make a bronze serpent and put it on a pole. Those who looked at it could save their lives after being bitten by a fiery serpent. God deemed their obedience to the word of Moses as faith and healed them.

It was not that fiery serpents that had previously not existed in the wilderness suddenly appeared. In the wilderness, there were not only serpents but also scorpions and insects that had poison. But because God protected them completely, those things could not touch the people. But when they complained and sinned, God could not protect them anymore and they were hurt.

Usually, when they face difficulties like accidents, diseases, or any kind of problem, people complain of their fate and consider it as coincidence. But when we have a problem, there always is a spiritual reason for it, just like the Israelites had to find the cause and solution from God about the problem of fiery serpents. And just like the sons of Israel repented of their sins and came before Moses, we have to repent of our sins and come before God. When we repent to destroy the wall of sin and live by the word of God, any kind of problem can be solved.

Here, looking at the bronze serpent on the pole is the symbolic representation of Jesus Christ, who would save us from the curse of the Law, as said in John 3:14-15, *"As Moses lifted up the serpent in the wilderness, even so must the Son of Man be lifted up; so that whoever believes will in Him have eternal life."*

Those who obeyed the word of God and looked at the bronze serpent were saved. Likewise, when those souls who were going the way of death look at Jesus on the cross and accept Him as the Savior, they will receive salvation. This is what the bronze serpent represented.

Conquering the East of Jordan and Balaam

Aaron was the spokesperson and older brother of Moses. He had been through the whole process of Exodus and as time passed, Aaron breathed his last at Mount Hor.

The forty years of time was almost up. The people were about to end their hardships in the wilderness and march into the Promised Land.

For this, the Israelites fought battles with Sihon, king of Amorites and Og, king of Bashan. They wanted to pass through their lands, but they didn't allow it and warfare broke out. But God was with the Israelites, and they were easily able to conquer the areas east of the Jordan.

The Israelites then went down south and camped in the plains of Moab on the eastern side of the Jordan.

When Israelites conquered the lands of Amorites and Bashanites, and camped in the plain of Moab, Balak, king of Moab, felt endangered. Being in great agony, he sent his messenger to Balaam who was living at Pethor, to curse the Israelites.

Balaam was a Gentile but he knew how to communicate with God. When he prayed asking what the will of God was, God answered him saying, *"Do not go with them; you shall not curse the people, for they [the sons of Israel] are blessed"* (Numbers 22:12).

So he refused the request of Balak king of Moab. But Balak prepared more gold and jewels and sent them to Balaam through more distinguished leaders than those sent previously. Balaam's heart was now shaken and he asked God's will again.

So, God let him go to the king of Moab. This was not the

case of God changing His mind. It was because God knew the changing heart of Balaam and his desires, and God just let Balaam do what he desired in his heart. God even opened the mouth of a donkey and let it speak to Balaam to make him understand that what he was doing was not right. But he did not turn back.

Of course, Balaam could not really curse the people of Israel even after going to Balak. Balak served Balaam very well and asked him to curse the Israelites from the high places of Baal. But Balaam blessed the Israelites instead by speaking the words given to him.

Balak asked Balaam to curse them three times changing the locations, but Balaam only blessed Israel.

> *How fair are your tents, O Jacob, Your dwellings, O Israel! Like valleys that stretch out, like gardens beside the river, like aloes planted by the LORD, like cedars beside the waters (Numbers 24:5-6).*

Balaam could not just speak against the will of God to curse the Israelites. But he still wanted the gifts and expensive things so he had an idea. He wanted to make the Israelites commit sins so that God would have to turn His face away from them.

So, when the Moabites were giving sacrifices to their gods,

Balaam made them invite the Israelites. The Israelites came to the land of Moab, and ate and drank and bowed before idols. They were tempted and seduced. They committed lewd and obscene acts with the women of Moab. This sin caused a plague which killed many people.

The Bible calls Balaam a person who went the way of death with his love for unrighteous wages and it warns us not to follow his example. Of course, it's not that Balaam disobeyed the will of God from the beginning. But he could not overcome the temptation of money and once his mind was captured, he finally became corrupted.

Today, there are many cases where people love money, compromise with the world, and commit sins before God. With their desire for money, they violate the commands of God. They don't keep the Lord's Day holy. They feel stingy about giving the proper tithes and eventually 'rob God.' But to compromise with the world and to love something else more than God is to commit spiritual adultery.

The foolish Balaam gained many things for the moment, but soon he faced a tragic end and was killed by the Israelites. Though it was delayed for a moment because of Balaam's wicked wisdom, Israel still conquered the part east of the Jordan. This land was taken by the tribes of Reuben, Gad, and part of the tribe of Manasseh upon their request.

Children at the time of Exodus had now grown up to become adults, and they were now playing the main role in leading Israel. All of the first generation of the Exodus, except for two, died in the wilderness because of their complaining against God at the Kadesh-Barnea. Moses and Aaron also could not go into the Canaan Land because, as the leaders, they had the responsibility for it.

Only Joshua and Caleb received the promise that they would go into the Land of Canaan with the next generation. Unlike other people who still had hardened hearts even after seeing so many miracles and died in the wilderness, they changed their hearts with the truth and increased in true faith.

They were not afraid even at the sight of the big people in Canaan and their strong fortresses. They confessed, *"If the LORD is pleased with us, then He will bring us into this land and give it to us—a land which flows with milk and honey"* (Numbers 14:8). This confession of Joshua and Caleb can also be applied to us today in the same way.

Let us realize that, if God is pleased with us, anything is possible for us. I hope you will ask with true faith and receive answers.

Chapter 5

"The LORD Your God Is with You"

- The Successor to Moses -

Joshua 1:6-9

Be strong and courageous, for you shall give this people possession of the land which I swore to their fathers to give them. Only be strong and very courageous; be careful to do according to all the law which Moses My servant commanded you; do not turn from it to the right or to the left, so that you may have success wherever you go. This book of the law shall not depart from your mouth, but you shall meditate on it day and night, so that you may be careful to do according to all that is written in it; for then you will make your way prosperous, and then you will have success. Have I not commanded you? Be strong and courageous! Do not tremble or be dismayed, for the LORD your God is with you wherever you go.

The forty years in the wilderness were not only a time of punishment for the Israelites who could not show faith, but it was also a time of spiritual training. It was a period for the second generation of the Exodus to meet God, experience Him, and gain faith.

God lets us go through various periods of training so that we can have spiritual faith first before He blesses us. Without spiritual faith we can neither be saved nor can we enter into the heavenly kingdom.

Also, if God gives us blessings before we have spiritual faith, then most of us would go back to the world. That is why God lets us see the amazing works of God and sometimes lets us go through fiery trials so that our faith can grow.

Of course, the period of time that a person has been Christian does not really matter for a person to receive spiritual and material blessings and to receive spiritual authority and power. It depends on the spiritual faith we possess. The spiritual faith can be given when we keep the word of God in our hearts and change our inner hear.

Only Moses, Joshua and Caleb survived together with the second generation. Everyone else in the first generation of the

Exodus died in the wilderness.

The Last Sermon of Moses

After the forty years, when it was the time to go into Canaan Land, Moses began to give a long sermon. It was just like a father who was giving the last will to his children with much concern about them. He was giving his final advice with great affection to the people of Israel who had to conquer the Land of Canaan after his death.

Actually, the entire content of the sermon is in the book of Deuteronomy. Deuteronomy is a message about the Law from the things that Moses taught the people of Israel on the plain of Moab.

Moses emphasized that the first generation of Exodus could not receive the Canaan Land as an inheritance because of their disobedience. He tried to bring them to an understanding that obedience to God is the passage to blessings and it is the most fundamental duty of men. Deuteronomy is a guide and textbook explaining the most basic principles and basic understanding that the people of God had to have. The key point is that they had to keep the commandments of God.

So you shall observe to do just as the LORD your God has commanded you; you shall not turn aside to the right or to the left. You shall walk in all the way which the LORD your God has commanded you, that you may live and that it may be well with you, and that you may prolong your days in the land which you will possess (Deuteronomy 5:32-33).

Now it shall be, if you diligently obey the LORD your God, being careful to do all His commandments which I command you today, the LORD your God will set you high above all the nations of the earth (Deuteronomy 28:1).

The theme repeated over and over again in Deuteronomy is that we will be blessed when we keep the commandments of God and we will be cursed if we don't. This was not given to make the people afraid or lay a burden on them. As said in Deuteronomy 10:13, *"Keep the LORD's commandments and His statutes which I am commanding you today for your good,"* it was the message telling them the way of true happiness.

Since the Fall of Adam, this world came under the control of the enemy devil. Those who don't believe in God are destined to suffer from tests and trials under Satan's control. Therefore, for us to live a blessed life, we have to depart from darkness and keep the word of God who is light.

1 John 1:6 says, *"If we say that we have fellowship with Him and yet walk in the darkness, we lie and do not practice*

the truth." Those who do not keep the commandments of God are those who dwell in darkness, and they belong to the enemy devil.

So, when the enemy devil brings tests and trials to such people, God cannot protect them. For example, there are the rules for traffic lights that are set by a country to ensure the safety of pedestrians and the flow of traffic. Both drivers and pedestrians can be protected when they obey the traffic light rules. On the other hand if one or the other goes against the lights, they cannot be protected.

In the same way, when we keep the law of God we can be protected, but otherwise, we cannot be protected. Moses knew this fact very well and advised the Israelites to keep the commandments of God many times.

Moses could not go into the Land of Canaan, but he blessed the sons of Israel (Deuteronomy chapter 33).

With his faith alone, he could have gone into the Canaan Land, but as the leader of the first generation of Exodus who did not have faith, he wasn't allowed to go into the land. It was because as the leader he was responsible (Deuteronomy 3:25-26). Generally, even in this world, some leaders or directors are relieved of their positions because of the mistakes of their subordinates. This is somewhat similar.

Before God took His beloved Moses, He showed Moses the Land of Canaan to comfort him. God loved Moses more than anybody else because he obeyed the will of God and guided numerous people with meekness. That is why God let him see the land from a distance, although he couldn't actually go into the land.

God guided him from the plains of Moab to Mount Nebo, and showed him all the land, Gilead as far as Dan, and all Naphtali and the land of Ephraim and Manasseh, and all the land of Judah as far as the western sea, and the Negev and the plain in the valley of Jericho, the city of palm trees, as far as Zoar (Deuteronomy 34:1-3).

What might Moses have felt seeing the Promised Land before his eyes? Because he believed the promise of God more firmly than anybody else, he probably felt sorry and somewhat embarrassed before God for not being able to guide the first generation of Exodus to have more faith.

He must have remembered the forty years that had passed since the moment he met God in a blazing fire from the midst of the bush on Mount Horeb. He might have also had lingering thoughts like, "If only I could have planted more faith in them." He was to leave earth by God's will, and he must have felt the burden and weight coming from his burning heart for the people who were remaining behind.

But some say Moses could not go into the Canaan Land because he didn't obey the word of God. They say that when Moses was to hit the rock to have water come out from it, he had to hit it only once but he hit it twice, and that is why God was angry with him. Or some others say he couldn't go into

Canaan Land because he had become so angry and he broke the tablets of the Ten Commandments.

But Numbers 12:3 says, *"Now the man Moses was very humble, more than any man who was on the face of the earth."* If this humble and gentle Moses could not go into the Canaan Land only because God's wrath fell on him for getting angry once, it sounds as though God is a very fearful God.

Also, we can find in the Bible that God just told him to hit the rock. Whether to hit it once or twice was up to Moses. We cannot say he disobeyed the word of God. The actual reason why Moses could not go into the Land was found in Deuteronomy 1:37. Moses said, *"The LORD was angry with me also on your account, saying, 'Not even you shall enter there.'"*

God made this verse be recorded in the Bible so that people would not have misunderstandings such as thinking it was because Moses got angry or he didn't have faith. It was not the case.

The Death of Moses

To the east of the Jordan, from where he could see the Canaan Land, Moses finally went to the side of the Father God after 120 years of life that was full of all kinds of unexpected changes.

Since he had received from God the duty of being the

leader of the Exodus, he obeyed all the words of God.

To become a leader was not an easy thing. He had to take on all the burdens and agonies of his people. He always had the concerns with the heart of a father to lead the people to follow the will of God.

Because of the people who were complaining with evil words, and because of the concerns and agonies he bore, he barely had any days of comfort until he was called to God's side.

But he never wanted to give up on his duty and never tried to shirk his responsibility. He only fell on the ground before God, humbly confessing he couldn't do anything with his own strength. He overcame all kinds of difficult situations only with his faith in God.

Because he had this kind of inner heart, God also trusted him, communicated directly with him, and let him accomplish so many great things.

Have you ever felt that your God-given duty is heavy and you just wanted to take a rest? I hope you will think about Moses and march on more vigorously.

Joshua, Successor to Moses

After Moses died, God chose Joshua, the son of Nun, to lead the people of Israel. Joshua was one of the twelve spies and he pleased God with his positive profession of faith.

He always followed Moses as his servant, and even when Moses fasted for forty days to receive the Ten Commandments, he did not leave Moses. Exodus 33:11 says, *"When Moses returned to the camp, his servant Joshua, the son of Nun, a young man, would not depart from the tent."* As said, he had love for the holy place of God.

Because Joshua loved God and trusted Moses with an unchanging heart, he could be chosen as the successor to Moses. He also probably had a great burden in his heart because the great leader was not with him anymore, and he now had to accept his teacher's responsibilities.

He knew how hard and burdensome the responsibility of leadership was for so many people. For forty years Joshua saw Moses' tears and agony more closely than anyone else. Because God knew this heart of Joshua, God encouraged him with strong words of promise.

> *No man will be able to stand before you all the days of your life. Just as I have been with Moses, I will be with you; I will not fail you or forsake you. Be strong and courageous, for you shall give this people possession of the land which I swore to their fathers to give them (Joshua 1:5-6).*

But, there was one condition. It was that he had to keep every word of God.

> *Only be strong and very courageous; be careful to do according to all the law which Moses My servant commanded you; do not turn from it to the right or to the left, so that you may have success wherever you go. This book of the law shall not depart from your mouth, but you shall meditate on it day and night, so that you may be careful to do according to all that is written in it; for then you will make your way prosperous, and then you will have success (Joshua 1:7-8).*

The Israelites who were with Joshua were also different from the first generation of the Exodus. Their parents' generation was born and raised in the gentile culture of the Egyptians and their faith in God was weak. A lot of evil was also planted in them since they were under the persecutions and maltreatment of slavery for so long. But the second generation was raised with the word of God and they had seen many powerful works of God from the time they were young.

Also, they had engraved in their hearts the reason why their parents could not go into the Canaan Land, and had to wander around in the wilderness for forty years. Now, they were ready to obey God and their leader with true faith.

Unlike their parents who did not cease to complain against Moses even after experiencing numerous works, they vowed to obey Joshua unconditionally.

> *Just as we obeyed Moses in all things, so we will obey you; only may the LORD your God be with you as He was with Moses. Anyone who rebels against your command and does not obey your words in all that you command him, shall be put to death; only be strong and courageous (Joshua 1:17-18).*

The leader, Joshua, and all the people were united in one heart to fulfill the promise of God concerning the Land of Canaan. Now, it was right before their eyes.

Canaan at that time had an advanced and high quality culture. They traded with Egypt and Mesopotamia. For the Israelites, who were once slaves and who also wandered around the wilderness for forty years, the Canaan Land was truly a land flowing with milk and honey.

The first place that they had to conquer to go into Canaan Land was Jericho.

Spying Out Jericho and Rahab the Harlot

Joshua and the Israelites didn't just march onto Jericho just because they had faith. They first had to know about their enemy. In order to form the right strategy they had to find out what their city walls were like, the strength of their armed forces, and how high their morale was. Joshua chose two spies at Shittim and sent them to scout the land.

The city of Jericho was a masterpiece at the time. When

we see the foundations of the city wall that the scholars have researched, we can see it was a very strong wall. Most cities have only one wall, but Jericho had two walls that made it much stronger.

It is known that the thickness of each wall was 1.8 meters and 3.3 meters respectively. It would have been difficult to make even a small hole in the city wall with just some ordinary means of attack. Especially the people in Jericho were on a high degree of caution, trying to defend themselves from an attack by the Israelites.

One day, the king of Jericho heard that spies had sneaked into the city. He had his soldiers search for them. They knew exactly where the spies were, and the spies could be caught any time.

At this moment, God provided a completely unexpected helping hand. It was Rahab, a harlot in whose house the spies were staying. She was a Gentile and from a low social position, but she hid the spies disobeying the king's order and made an amazing confession of faith to them.

> [Rahab] said to the men, "I know that the LORD has given you the land, and that the terror of you has fallen on us, and that all the inhabitants of the land have melted away before you. For we have heard how the LORD dried up the water of the Red Sea before you when you came out of Egypt, and what you did to the two kings of the

Amorites who were beyond the Jordan, to Sihon and Og, whom you utterly destroyed. When we heard it, our hearts melted and no courage remained in any man any longer because of you; for the LORD your God, He is God in heaven above and on earth beneath" (Joshua 2:9-11).

Though Rahab was a Gentile woman, she had a good heart. When she heard about the parting of the Red Sea into two, water coming out from a rock, and the victories of Israel in battles, she believed in the almighty God.

So she asked that the spies spare her life and the lives of her family members, just as she spared their lives, when the Israelites would conquer the city of Jericho.

With human thoughts we may think she betrayed her own people and hid enemy spies. But what she chose was not one nation over another, but she chose the almighty God the Creator.

When they heard about the signs and wonders of God that accompanied the Israelites, even Gentiles who had good hearts acknowledged God in heaven above and on earth beneath.

God does not ever forsake but gives blessings to those who seek Him and rely on Him with true hearts, for He searches the deep heart.

The Profession of Faith of the Two Spies

The spies escaped from the city with the help of Rahab and hid themselves in the mountains for three days. They then crossed the Jordan River again to go back to the camp of Israel. What do you think they said to Joshua?

They made a detailed report about the land they had seen. They did not say anything with negative attitudes or fear. They only confessed what they had seen with the eyes of faith.

> *Surely the LORD has given all the land into our hands; moreover, all the inhabitants of the land have melted away before us (Joshua 2:24).*

We can see this profession was so different from the ten spies at Kadesh-Barnea. If we truly believe in God, there is nothing impossible. Even problems will turn into prosperity if God is with us. So, we should not say anything negative like, "It's impossible!" or "It's too difficult." People commonly say many negative and dishonest things because it's become a habit of speech in their lives.

For example, they say things like, "I am dying to see it," "It's killing me," "That tastes good enough to die for!" "I'm so full I could just burst!" Such exaggerated and untrue utterances are commonplace.

God sees all our words, deeds, and inner heart and works according to the faith. Proverbs 18:20-21 says, *"With the fruit of a man's mouth his stomach will be satisfied; he will be satisfied with the product of his lips. Death and life are in the power of the tongue, and those who love it will eat its fruit."*

Therefore, we should speak words of faith and goodness and positive words so we can encourage others and plant faith in them, too.

Chapter 6

They Cross the Jordan on Dry Ground

- Jordan River Stops -

Joshua 3:14-17

So when the people set out from their tents to cross the Jordan with the priests carrying the ark of the covenant before the people, and when those who carried the ark came into the Jordan, and the feet of the priests carrying the ark were dipped in the edge of the water (for the Jordan overflows all its banks all the days of harvest), the waters which were flowing down from above stood and rose up in one heap, a great distance away at Adam, the city that is beside Zarethan; and those which were flowing down toward the sea of the Arabah, the Salt Sea, were completely cut off. So the people crossed opposite Jericho. And the priests who carried the ark of the covenant of the LORD stood firm on dry ground in the middle of the Jordan while all Israel crossed on dry ground, until all the nation had finished crossing the Jordan.

The second generation of Exodus, led by Joshua, began their march towards the Canaan Land. Because of the mission report from the spies concerning Jericho, the morale of the people of Israel was soaring as they vigorously advanced on the city.

The hearts of the people in Canaan had already melted away, and they didn't have to wait any longer. From early morning Joshua made the people get ready and then they moved to the Jordan River.

Flooding the Jordan River

On the way to Jericho the swift current of the flooding Jordan River was blocking them. So Joshua didn't cross the river right away with his people, but he had them set up camp there for a while.

They had to find a way to cross the river because it was the season for the flooding of the river and it had a very strong flow.

The width of the river has decreased over a period of time, and now it's only about thirty meters in width, but at that time it was considerably wider.

Just in case of the Yellow River, which is also known as the Hwang Ho in China, it changes the course of its flow over a period of time. Along the river there are some villages that completely disappear and others that are newly established over time. So, about 3,500 years ago the Jordan River must have been very different from the river that it is today.

Also, the Jordan had many sharp bends and a fast current. It was also the time of harvest when the Jordan overflows all its banks (Joshua 3:15).

When there is sudden shower during the summer, even little valley streams overflow and those rapid flows even cause deaths of people.

It was impossible for more than two million people together with the children and elderly people, and their baggage to cross a big river when it was flooding. Even if they wanted to build ships or a bridge, they couldn't get the materials. Even if they could, it would have taken a long time. The people in Jericho wouldn't have just watched them either.

The Faith of the Second Generation of the Exodus

Unlike the first generation of the Exodus, the second generation was well trained and had the spiritual faith to rely on the almighty God.

When the flooding Jordan River was blocking their way, God taught them a very simple way to cross it.

He told them that if the priests would step into the flooding Jordan River carrying the ark of the covenant, the water would stop flowing and it would pile up in a heap. Using only common sense this was impossible. How could the flow of river stop just by stepping on it?

If the first generation of the Exodus had been asked to step into the Jordan River with the ark of the covenant, they wouldn't have kept quiet about it. They would have immediately started complaining and saying, "Go into the flooding river with the Ark! Are we supposed to die just like that? Has God guided us all the way here from Egypt just to kill us in the Jordan River?"

However the second generation did not utter a single word of complaint or doubt. God had already divided the Red Sea into two. They believed that, for such God, stopping the flow of the Jordan River was not a problem.

The Jordan River Stops

Before they crossed the Jordan, once more Joshua made a request of the nation of Israel.

> *Consecrate yourselves, for tomorrow the LORD will do wonders among you (Joshua 3:5).*

The next day, according to the word of God that was passed on by Joshua to the people, the priests carried the ark of the covenant and went on ahead of the people and stood by the River.

At the beginning of the Exodus, when the Red Sea was divided and the Egyptian army was buried in it, it was done solely by the obedience of one person Moses. Although they had seen the power of God demonstrated through the Ten Plagues inflicted on Egypt, at that time the Israelites didn't have enough faith.

But now, before the flooding Jordan River, the faith of not just one person, Joshua, but the faith of everyone in Israel was necessary. In much the same way, from the time we accept Jesus Christ, we have to grow up in spirit and show deeds of faith. They had to obey the word of Joshua who was appointed by God and step into the flow of the Jordan River.

The instant that the priests stepped into the flowing river, the promise of God was fulfilled as spoken. The waters which were flowing down from above stood still and rose up in one heap (Joshua 3:16), and those which were flowing down toward the sea of the Arabah, the Salt Sea, were completely cut off.

While the priests were standing on the bed of the river with the ark of the covenant, the water didn't flow and the Israelites quickly crossed the river. When the priests came up out of the river, the water began to flow again like before.

As the Israelites witnessed this great power of God, they came to trust Joshua even more and began to revere him as they had revered Moses.

A Commemoration with Twelve Stones

God wanted them to remember that day forever and not to change in their reverence toward God, and He commanded them to do something. God told them to take up twelve stones from the middle of the Jordan according to the number of the tribes of the sons of Israel and they had to carry them over with them to the lodging place and put them down there.

God also had them set up twelve stones in the middle of the Jordan at the place where the feet of the priests who carried the ark of the covenant were standing. It was for them to remember forever what God had done for Israel, and to revere and obey God.

> *[Joshua] said to the sons of Israel, "When your children ask their fathers in time to come, saying, 'What are these stones?' then you shall inform your children, saying, 'Israel crossed this Jordan on dry ground. For the LORD your God dried up the waters of the Jordan before you until you had crossed, just as the LORD your God had done to the Red Sea, which He dried up before us until we had crossed; that all the peoples of the earth may know that the hand of the LORD is mighty, so that you may fear the LORD your God forever'" (Joshua 4:21-24).*

God confirmed once again that He is with the Israelites through the amazing work of stopping the Jordan River. On the other hand, after hearing this news the Canaanites were so afraid that their hearts melted and there was no spirit in them any longer.

> *Now it came about when all the kings of the Amorites who were beyond the Jordan to the west, and all the kings of the Canaanites who were by the sea, heard how the LORD had dried up the waters of the Jordan before the sons of Israel until they had crossed, that their hearts melted, and there was no spirit in them any longer because of the sons of Israel (Joshua 5:1).*

Israelites had very high spirits and it seemed that they could conquer the city of Jericho immediately. But God did not let them attack Jericho right away. He made them do something first.

Before such a major attack God did not tell them to get their weapons and soldiers ready for battle. He commanded them to circumcise themselves.

The Spiritual Meaning of Circumcision

The physical act of circumcision is to cut off the male's foreskin on the eighth day of birth. It was first commanded to Abraham.

In Genesis chapter 17, God promised Abraham that He would give him the Canaan Land. With the promise, God commanded him to circumcise the men. He said, *"This is My covenant, which you shall keep, between Me and you and your descendants after you: every male among you shall be circumcised"* (Genesis 17:10).

From this time the sons of Israel were circumcised on the eighth day of their birth. It was the symbol of covenant that Israel is the people of God. God commanded them to keep it throughout generations, and those who were not circumcised had to be cut off from the people of God.

This command is applied in the same way to us in the New Testament times. But it is not physical but spiritual circumcision. We have to circumcise our hearts (Deuteronomy 10:16). Circumcision of heart is commanded in Jeremiah 4:4, *"Circumcise yourselves to the LORD and remove the foreskins of your heart."*

To remove the foreskins of heart is to obey the commands of God telling us 'to do,' 'not to do,' 'to keep,' or 'to cast away' certain things as spoken. Namely, as God says, it is 'to love'; 'not to hate'; 'to keep the Sabbath'; and to 'cast off all forms of evil.' To become sanctified we have to 'cast off' untruth, evil, unrighteousness, lawlessness, and darkness which are things that are against the word of God and we must 'keep' the truth.

In the times of the Old Testament they had the symbol of belonging to God by circumcision because it was not the time of the Holy Spirit and people could not cast away sins by their own strength. In the New Testament times, circumcision of heart is the sign of being God's children.

Therefore, just as those who were not circumcised in the Old Testament times were cut off from the people of God, circumcision of heart in the New Testament times is directly related with salvation.

Joshua had to conduct the circumcision because the sons of Israel who stayed in the wilderness from the time of the Exodus could not do the circumcision. They circumcised themselves just before the Exodus, and those who were born in the wilderness, namely those men under the age of forty were not circumcised.

So, before the conquering of Canaan began in full scale, God made all men receive circumcision to confirm His covenant once again.

This was not a simple matter. Once they had been circumcised, they would have pain and would not be able to move freely for several days. Especially, since they had already crossed the Jordan River, they were already in the range of attack by their enemies. The people in Jericho were carefully watching them at a very close proximity.

If they had circumcised themselves and the enemy attacked them, they would have been defeated without being able to fight back. So, with a human way of thinking, they may have thought, "Why didn't God let us be circumcised in the wilderness instead? Why has He commanded us to do it in this dangerous situation?" They could have complained or even disobeyed with such thoughts.

Sometimes, God commands us to do something that is impossible by human thought. But, thinking something is impossible is fleshly thought and that is what blocks us from experiencing the amazing works of God. It is the primary factor that cuts off or diminishes the power of God that can be brought down to us.

But because the Israelites of the second generation of the Exodus had faith, they just obeyed without saying anything. As a result, God protected them until their cuts were completely healed, and no enemy force came near them.

Circumcision and Spiritual Battle

Then, what is the reason that God commanded them to circumcise themselves in such a dangerous situation? This was to teach not only the Israelites but everyone, including us today, how to win spiritual battles.

The process of conquering the Land of Canaan may be seen as merely fighting over land among different peoples, but in spiritual realm, it was fierce spiritual battle for victory and defeat between good spirits belonging to God and evil spirits that tried to disgrace God.

For our struggle is not against flesh and blood, but against the rulers, against the powers, against the world forces of this darkness, against the spiritual forces of wickedness in the heavenly places (Ephesians 6:12).

For example, when the boy David defeated Goliath, he said, *"And that all this assembly may know that the LORD does not deliver by sword or by spear; for the battle is the LORD's and He will give you into our hands"* (1 Samuel 17:47).

The small body of the boy, David, could not begin to compare with the massive body and great strength of Goliath, but David won because he was a man after God's heart. Because he had already won the spiritual battle, he was able to defeat the giant Goliath with just a sling and a stone.

Also, in the battle between Israel and Amalek after the Exodus, when Moses' hands were raised, Israel prevailed, and when he let his hands down, Amalek prevailed (Exodus 17:11). When the man of God, Moses, raised his hands and prayed, God was with them to prevail in the battle.

There are many other verses in the Bible in addition to these that tell us that the victory in a battle does not depend on the physical fight but spiritual battle (Genesis 32:24-25; Daniel 10:13).

For example, suppose somebody is persecuted at home or workplace because she is a believer. On the outside, her parents, husband, or boss in the workplace persecute her, but in spirit, it is actually the evil spirits that incite the people to give a hard time to her.

Those who do not know Jesus Christ and have not accepted Him belong to Satan the ruler of this dark world. So, the evil spirits can stimulate these people to have negative thoughts.

In this situation, if the believer pleases God and receives His power, she can receive the help of angels and heavenly host. Thus the evil spirits will lose their power and the minds of the persecutors will also be calmed down naturally.

This battle of Joshua and the sons of Israel against Jericho was also a spiritual battle under God's control. That is why the captain of the host of God came to Joshua as he neared Jericho.

> *Now it came about when Joshua was by Jericho, that he lifted up his eyes and looked, and behold, a man was standing opposite him with his sword drawn in his hand, and Joshua went to him and said to him, "Are you for us or for our adversaries?" He said, "No; rather I indeed come now as captain of the host of the LORD." And Joshua fell on his face to the earth, and bowed down, and said to him, "What has my lord to say to his servant?" (Joshua 5:13-14)*

There is something that is absolutely necessary to win this kind of spiritual battle. It is the purity of heart.

This is the reason why God commanded them to sanctify themselves before they crossed the Jordan River.

The captain of the host of the LORD told Joshua to remove his sandals from his feet (Joshua 5:15), and it was for the same reason as above, to spiritually remove the filth of sin and achieve the purity of sanctification.

Before the fulfillment of the promise of God to give them the Land of Canaan, God let them circumcise themselves first. It was to let them cast off sins and purify themselves once again.

1 John 3:21-22 also says, *"Beloved, if our heart does not condemn us, we have confidence before God; and whatever we ask we receive from Him, because we keep His commandments and do the things that are pleasing in His sight."*

Thus, not only in conquering the Canaan Land but also in personal matter, we first have to circumcise our heart by casting off evil from the heart, so that God can show His work.

Now, between the Israelites who had just circumcised themselves and the people in Jericho, there was great tension, like just before a storm.

But God had already sent His heavenly army for this battle and promised Joshua saying, *"See, I have given Jericho into your hand, with its king and the valiant warriors"* (Joshua 6:2). Even the strong city of Jericho was already in God's hands.

> *Indeed, ask now concerning the former days which were before you, since the day that God created man on the earth, and inquire from one end of the heavens to the other. Has anything been done like this great thing, or has anything been heard like it? (Deuteronomy 4:32)*

Who can divide a sea to make a way through it? Who can stop the flow of a flooded river, open the gate of heaven to give daily food, and make water spring out from a rock? Only the almighty God can do these things.

These are not just things of the imagination, myths, or legends. They are purely historical facts containing no fabrications.

Therefore, just like the priests who stepped in the river carrying the ark of the covenant and without fearing what is seen with the eyes, we should be able to boldly stand up, step out and work for the glory of God.

Chapter 7

"The LORD Has Given You the City"

- The Conquest of Jericho -

Joshua 6:12; 15-16

Now Joshua rose early in the morning, and the priests took up the ark of the LORD. ...

Then on the seventh day they rose early at the dawning of the day and marched around the city in the same manner seven times; only on that day they marched around the city seven times. At the seventh time, when the priests blew the trumpets, Joshua said to the people, "Shout! For the LORD has given you the city."

All along the city wall encircling Jericho it was dead quiet. Jericho was the gateway to the Land of Canaan and a big city. There had to have been many people moving around, but it was very quiet.

> Now Jericho was tightly shut because of the sons of Israel; no one went out and no one came in (Joshua 6:1).

The people inside the city were silently waiting for the inevitable battle with the Israelites and paying close attention to their every move.

God's Way of Conquering the City of Jericho

It was clear that people in Jericho had the advantage over the Israelites. They were within the strong city walls while Israelites were in the field with no way to retreat since the Jordan River was behind them.

Common sense tells us that Israel would obviously be defeated, but God said they would win. Joshua 6:2 says, *"The LORD said to Joshua, 'See, I have given Jericho into your hand, with its king and the valiant warriors.'"*

If they had modern weapons of today, the city wall wouldn't be a problem. But they didn't even have gunpowder. The city of Jericho had an inner wall and an outer wall. It was so strong that even chariots would run on top of the walls. It was heavily guarded by armed soldiers. There just was no way to conquer it with the strength of the sons of Israel alone.

In this situation, God taught them a method that was not easily understood with common sense. He told them to march around the city once for six days and then seven times on the seventh day.

At the front were the armed men followed by the seven priests with seven rams' horn trumpets, then the men carrying the ark of the LORD immediately behind them, and then the people of the nation of Israel who marched behind the ark of the LORD. On the seventh day, when they would march around the city seven times and the priests would blow the trumpets, the people would then shout and the city of Jericho would collapse.

Here, the number seven, which repeatedly appears, is the number of perfection. This means they had to believe in God completely and obey Him. God told them that when the people would shout with the priests blowing the trumpets, the city wall would fall, and this spiritually implies that God's will is for us to cry out to God.

Call to Me and I will answer you, and I will tell you great and mighty things, which you do not know (Jeremiah 33:3).

We can see in the Bible that the prophets and Jesus' disciples cried out with loud voices in their prayers. When Jesus revived the dead Lazarus, He 'cried out with a loud voice' saying, "Lazarus, come forth." The man who had died came forth, bound hands and feet with wrappings, and his face was wrapped around with a cloth (John 11:43-44).

When Jesus called forth a dead man, a loud voice or soft voice would have been the same. But, because He was praying before the living God, He cried out in a loud voice. This is also the reason why He prayed until His sweat became like drops of blood falling down upon the ground when He was praying at Gethsemane just before taking the cross (Luke 22:44).

Just as we can eat the harvest of the ground with our toil (Genesis 3:17), we can receive the answer to our prayer more quickly when we toil and cry out in prayer. Likewise, it is the will of God for us to cry out in prayer when we ask for something before God.

Sons of Israel Conquered Jericho with Faith

Such strong city walls as those of Jericho fell down by people's shouts? It is absolutely impossible and incomprehensible with human thoughts. But the second generation of the Exodus had gone through the training of faith and they did not make any negative remarks nor did they complain; they just obeyed.

Now, the people in the city of Jericho saw something very strange. They got ready to fight as the entire army and all the people of the nation of Israel seemed to come to attack them. But they just marched around the city once and went back to their camp.

On the second day as well, the Israelites did not even throw a stone at them. They just marched around the city once and went back. They continued to do it for six days. How dumb-founded and puzzled the people of Jericho must have been! They were so puzzled by the strategy that could not be comprehended that they did not even consider shooting an arrow at the people of Israel.

The people in Jericho became increasingly nervous watching the Israelites so boldly marching around the city wall with the trumpets that they couldn't even think of attacking them.

If they had attacked, things could have been different. But they were so afraid of the Israelites who crossed the Jordan River by God's work that they could not move at all. They must have been thinking that the Israelites had some kind of special strategy. It was because God had made them fear the Israelites to the point they could not do anything but just watch the incomprehensible acts of the Israelites.

However on the seventh day, their actions changed. They started to march around the city from early morning. They marched around seven times. Then after the priests blew the trumpets, Joshua gave a signal.

Shout! For the LORD has given you the city (Joshua 6:16).

When the people began to shout loudly at the signal given by Joshua, something truly amazing took place. The double city walls that seemed to be impregnable together with so many soldiers began to collapse in a moment.

Just imagine this astonishing scene.

It is impossible for any city wall or building to collapse without some kind of a shock or pressure applied to it. But these double city walls, of which one was 1.8 meters and the other 3.3 meters thick, just fell down without having laid a finger on it.

By the shout of the people of Israel, the city wall turned into piles of rocks with a collapsing roar and so much dust covered the sky. Inside the city was chaos. With the screaming of those who were crushed by the broken wall, the people and soldiers inside were just running here and there. The sons of Israel were able to conquer this city very easily.

In our lives we may encounter problems that seem like the impregnable city of Jericho. Even when there seems to be no solution, those with strong willpower will try their best to solve the problems. But even those people are helpless with the problems that are beyond human ability. Finally, they will fall and collapse in discouragement.

But those children of God who have faith have nothing to worry about. They believe even the things that are impossible by men are possible by the power of God. They will discern what the will of God is and act with faith. Then, God will solve all their problems like He stopped the Jordan River and destroyed the city of Jericho.

Psalm 20:7 says, *"Some boast in chariots and some in horses, but we will boast in the name of the LORD, our God."* As written, if we do not rely on the worldly methods of knowledge, but rely on God and march on with faith, God will fight for us and lead us.

God's Justice and the Conquering of Jericho

The sons of Israel did not take any loot in the city personally. They burned some and offered some other things to God. Because it was something that they gained for the first time in the Promised Land, they gave it to God. This is like we give the first fruit of our income to God.

With the exceptions of Rahab, who had saved the two Israelite spies, and her family, the Israelites killed every person and every animal in Jericho. Some may say it was cruel to kill all the people in the city, but there was a reason for doing it.

It was necessary for them to kill every person and every animal in the city of Jericho in order to keep the holiness of the Israelites. The people in Canaan were living a completely corrupted and sinful life-style. In particular, they were playing the harlot worshipping idols.

If the sons of Israel had let them live and dwelled among them, they would have been stained with sins and finally they would have fallen into death. For this reason God had no other choice but to allow the killing of all the people in Jericho.

> *You shall consume all the peoples whom the LORD your God will deliver to you; your eye shall not pity them, nor shall you serve their gods, for that would be a snare to you (Deuteronomy 7:16).*

Those who do not understand this situation may think the conquering of the Land of Canaan is something unjust. It's because there were already people living in that land, but God took their land and just gave it to Israel, and He even commanded Israel to kill everyone in that land.

But the conquering of the Land of Canaan was not just to give that land to the Israelites. It was also a result of righteous punishment on the Canaanites who were living in overflowing sins.

In Genesis chapter 15, God prophesied to Abraham that

the people of Israel would enter into the Canaan Land. They would be enslaved in Egypt and then come back, and it was not the time yet. God said it was because, *"The iniquity of the Amorite is not yet complete"* (v. 16).

Within the justice of God, if the sin of a people reaches a certain limit, God must pass judgment and there is no option but punishment. It's because if the sin is left untreated, it will spread quickly like a contagious disease.

Examples of these cases are the punishment of fire and brimstone on Sodom and Gomorrah, the flood of Noah's time, and the destruction of Pompeii.

The whole city of Pompeii was covered by a very sudden volcanic eruption. When we see the remains, we can see that people in the city were so religiously and morally corrupted that they had to be punished.

It was thousands of years ago, but God had given Moses commandments prohibiting intercourse or mating with animals and homosexuality (Leviticus 18:22-23, 20:13-16). It tells us that there were such things at that time.

The Bible also records that those who served Molech, Baal, or Ashera did harm to themselves, burned their children as sacrifices, and committed adulterous acts before the idols (Exodus 34:15; Leviticus 18:21, 20:5; Deuteronomy 31:16).

Likewise, the Canaanites were also so corrupted that they had to be punished. In the method of punishment it was different from Sodom and Gomorrah or Pompeii; they were destroyed by the sons of Israel, God's elect. Nevertheless, God did not punish them immediately. He waited patiently and gave them many chances until finally their sins prevailed to the point He had to punish them. Until the very end He gave them many chances to change.

For example, at the time of Jonah the prophet, God commanded him to go to the city of Nineveh to proclaim the punishment of God so that they could repent. Although it was the capital city of Assyria, which was a hostile country toward Israel, when the people in Nineveh repented of their sins, God gave them grace and did not destroy the city.

> *The LORD is compassionate and gracious, slow to anger and abounding in lovingkindness (Psalm 103:8).*

God gave the people of Jericho many chances and endured with them for a long time, but they did not repent. Finally they had to be destroyed.

The Salvation of Rahab and Her Family

There is one more incident in particular by which we can feel the mercy and compassion of God. It was Rahab the harlot who helped two spies sent to scout the city. When Rahab heard about the works of God shown through Israel, she believed in God and hid the spies.

And they promised her that they would save her and

her family when they conquered Jericho, but there was one condition. She had to tie the cord of scarlet thread, which was used for the escape of the messengers, in her window, and she and her family had to stay inside the house. This was the condition for them to be protected in the chaos of the war.

This was somewhat similar with the plague and deaths of the firstborn at the time of the Exodus. When all the firstborns of Egypt were killed overnight, none of the firstborn of Israel was killed. At that time too there was a condition. They had to put the blood of the Lamb on two doorposts and lintel, and they had to stay inside the house for God to protect them.

This spiritually tells us the principle through which God's children are protected from disasters of this world. Today, sins are prevailing and there are many kinds of calamities. So many people suffer from and die in wars, famine, earthquakes, typhoons and hurricanes, floods, and various diseases.

But through the precious blood of Jesus, God's children are kept by God not to face any disasters. The condition is that they have to stay within the precious blood of Jesus. The Israelites put the blood on the doorposts and lintel and did not go outside, and likewise Rahab and her family put the cord of scarlet threat in the window and did not go outside. In the same way, to be protected we have to live in the word of God and we must not go outside the word befriending the world.

1 John 3:24 says, *"The one who keeps His commandments abides in Him, and He in him. We know by this that He abides in us, by the Spirit whom He has given us."* When we keep the commandments, the Lord can be with us and we can be protected all the time. Today, there are many believers, but they still suffer from tests and trials because they do not understand this point.

> *If you will give earnest heed to the voice of the LORD your God, and do what is right in His sight, and give ear to His commandments, and keep all His statutes, I will put none of the diseases on you which I have put on the Egyptians; for I, the LORD, am your healer (Exodus 15:26).*

Though Rahab was a prostitute, God kept such a person from punishment because she had a good heart and feared Him. Furthermore, because of the one person Rahab, the lives of her parents, brothers and sisters, and relatives could be saved.

Also, Rahab was a Gentile woman, but she received the blessing to be put in the genealogy of Jesus by her faith in God. God guided these good-hearted people to salvation even in a situation where He had to punish the city of Jericho because of their sins.

Prophecy of Joshua about Reconstruction of Jericho

There was another amazing incident related to Jericho. After he destroyed Jericho by the command of God, Joshua swore that Jericho would never be built again.

> *Cursed before the LORD is the man who rises up and builds this city Jericho; with the loss of his firstborn he shall lay its foundation, and with the loss of his youngest son he shall set up its gates (Joshua 6:26).*

Joshua's word was so surely guaranteed by God that it was fulfilled as said at the time of King Ahab, about 500 years later.

1 Kings 16:34 says, *"In his days Hiel the Bethelite built Jericho; he laid its foundations with the loss of Abiram his firstborn, and set up its gates with the loss of his youngest son Segub, according to the word of the LORD, which He spoke by Joshua the son of Nun."*

Men may forget or their memory may diminish through the passage of time, but God's word never changes even with the passage of time, and He guarantees the words of His prophets.

Chapter 8

"They Have Transgressed My Covenant"

- The Sin of Achan -

Joshua 7:10-13

So the LORD said to Joshua, "Rise up! Why is it that you have fallen on your face? Israel has sinned, and they have also transgressed My covenant which I commanded them. And they have even taken some of the things under the ban and have both stolen and deceived. Moreover, they have also put them among their own things. Therefore the sons of Israel cannot stand before their enemies; they turn their backs before their enemies, for they have become accursed. I will not be with you anymore unless you destroy the things under the ban from your midst. Rise up! Consecrate the people and say, 'Consecrate yourselves for tomorrow, for thus the LORD, the God of Israel, has said, "There are things under the ban in your midst, O Israel. You cannot stand before your enemies until you have removed the things under the ban from your midst."'"

Through their victory in Jericho, the sons of Israel became full of morale and they marched towards the city of Ai. But at the time they neglected something. They did not conquer the city of Jericho because of their great ability, but because God was with them.

Then later, when they attacked Ai, they should not have just attacked the city relying on their personal opinions, but they should have learned the will of God first. But because Ai was a small city, they just relied on their own strength and abilities.

The Defeat at Ai

The messengers who spied out the city of Ai told Joshua, *"Do not let all the people go up; only about two or three thousand men need go up to Ai; do not make all the people toil up there, for they are few."* Because they conquered the impregnable Jericho easily, they thought Ai would be no problem for them.

Of course, if it had been a very difficult matter like conquering Jericho, they would have asked God first, but they thought they could just conquer the city of Ai with their own strength. It was here that Joshua made a critical mistake.

Without trying to know the will of God, he just made a decision after hearing only the report of the messengers. When they crossed the Jordan River and conquered Jericho, they listened to God, but this time he only listened to men.

Hearing the report of the messengers, only three thousand men went up to fight, and Israel was brutally defeated. They were chased by the people of Ai, and thirty-six of them died in the battle.

They thought God was with them and they would certainly win, but they suffered only casualties without actually conquering the small city Ai. It was a great shock to them. It wasn't merely a defeat; it was a big problem because God was not with them any more.

That is why Joshua 7:5 says, *"The men of Ai struck down about thirty-six of their men, and pursued them from the gate as far as Shebarim and struck them down on the descent, so the hearts of the people melted and became as water."*

Just because the Israelites had crossed the Jordan River and conquered the city of Jericho, it didn't mean that the conquering of the Canaan Land was complete. In the continuous battles that were to follow, they had to be on alert and receive the help of God.

Usually, even in this world when people do something great, they act discretely with firm determination in the beginning, but once they overcome some difficult situations, their minds become more relaxed. They become lazy or proud and finally they fail.

The reason why Israelites could cross the Jordan River and conquer the strong city of Jericho so easily was not because their ability was great, but because God was with them. They forgot this fact and were defeated so badly in the battle with the small city of Ai.

The Sin of Achan

Joshua tore his clothes and fell to the earth on his face before the ark of the LORD until the evening, both he and the elders of Israel; and they put dust on their heads. He repented before God taking responsibility as the leader.

> O LORD, what can I say since Israel has turned their back before their enemies? For the Canaanites and all the inhabitants of the land will hear of it, and they will surround us and cut off our name from the earth. And what will You do for Your great name? (Joshua 7:8-9)

Because they knew God was with them, Israel could be brave before their enemies and that is why the Canaanites were afraid of them. But when they saw they were defeated at Ai, they felt that it was a sure indication that God had turned His back on Israel. If God had abandoned Israel, there would have been no other course for them but their annihilation by the enemy at the center of the field of battle.

Joshua tore his heart and pleaded with God for he did not understand why such a thing happened and what he had to do. Likewise, if we have any problem at home, at workplace, or at business, we should understand that there is a problem with us. We have to check ourselves and find out what was wrong in the sight of God and repent of it.

When Joshua fell on the earth before the ark of the LORD with the elders of Israel, God told him the reason for Israel's defeat.

God told the Israelites to offer to God everything they gained from Jericho, the first city they conquered, but somebody among the sons of Israel disobeyed (Joshua 7:11-12). God also said He could not be with Israel until they solved this problem.

Here, God did not directly tell them who that person was but told them to find him by a system of drawing lots.

Joshua conveyed the command of God to the people and told them to consecrate themselves. It was a little too late since they had already lost a battle, but they still had to turn away and solve the problem of sin among the sons of Israel.

> *Rise up! Consecrate the people and say, "Consecrate yourselves for tomorrow, for thus the LORD, the God of Israel, has said, 'There are things under the ban in your midst, O Israel. You cannot stand before your enemies until you have removed the things under the ban from your midst'" (Joshua 7:13).*

Next morning, when they cast lots among all the tribes of Israel, the tribe of Judah was selected. Next, among the tribe of Judah, the family of Zerahites was selected, and from them, the men of Zabdi. Finally, Achan was selected among the men of Zabdi.

The probability of being selected by the casting lots is the same for everybody. If we cast lots for one hundred people, the probability of being selected is 1/100. But God accurately selected this one man, Achan, who sinned from among a couple million people.

Proverbs 16:33 says, *"The lot is cast into the lap, but its every decision is from the LORD."* It was not a coincidence but the work of God Himself. Thus, since then, the people of Israel often cast lot when they did something in God's name.

Namely, these cases were when they were distributing the Land of Canaan, when Jonah met with a big storm while he was running away to Tarshish in disobedience to God's word, and when they selected the replacing disciple in place of Judas Iscariot (Joshua 18:10, 19:51; Jonah 1:7; Acts 1:26).

Just by seeing the process of revealing the sin of Achan, we can understand once again that God knows everything so clearly and He is in control of everything.

Then Joshua said to Achan, "My son, I implore you, give glory to the LORD, the God of Israel, and give praise

> to Him; and tell me now what you have done. Do not hide it from me" (Joshua 7:19).

> When I saw among the spoil a beautiful mantle from Shinar and two hundred shekels of silver and a bar of gold fifty shekels in weight, then I coveted them and took them; and behold, they are concealed in the earth inside my tent with the silver underneath it (Joshua 7:21).

Achan was inevitably selected by the lot commanded by God. When Joshua asked him to tell the truth, he couldn't hide what he had done and confessed that he had concealed what he had taken in the earth inside his tent.

Through this, we have to remember that God was not with the whole people of Israel because of the sin of one person. In Ecclesiastes 9:18, the latter part says, *"But one sinner destroys much good."*

Even today sometimes the entire organization has to take the responsibility for what one of the members did wrong. Corruption of one civil servant brings down the name of all of the civil servants. In the military, an entire unit of soldiers may receive some kind of punishment as a result of the wrongdoing of one person.

What God wanted was complete sanctification of all Israel and complete obedience. If one person disobeyed, it could cause God to leave Israel as a whole.

The City of Ai Conquered

To resolve this problem, Israel had to destroy the traces of sin completely and break down the wall of sin that was standing between them and God. Joshua told them to take Achan with the silver, the mantle, and the bar of gold that he had taken along with his family, animals, and all his possessions to the valley of Achor. All Israel stoned him and all the things with him and burned them. They raised over him a great heap of stones, and therefore the name of that place has been called the 'valley of Achor' to this day.

One may think that it was too cruel to give him such a punishment just for stealing a mantle and some silver and gold. But, in Exodus 22 we see the punishment for stealing. A thief has to compensate two times more amount of what he has stolen, or according to the object that was stolen, he has to pay back four to five times more.

But here, Achan's sin was not just simple stealing. He stole what was exclusively set apart for God. It implies he did not fear God at all, which means he took the name of God in vain and did not believe in Him. Only after Israel solved the problem of sin did God tell them in detail how to attack the city of Ai (Joshua chapter 8).

The strategy given to Israel by God was essentially that Israel had to pretend that they were being defeated and retreat while still engaged in the fighting so that they could draw the enemy force out of the city of Ai. Then, other Israelite soldiers who were hiding in ambush near the city were to enter into the city, conquer it, and burn it.

Joshua followed the word of God. He ambushed some soldiers to the west of the city, and he led some other soldiers to join with him to fight to the north of the city. Soon, they began to retreat. Since the people in Ai had won a victory already, they were careless enough to leave their city gates wide open to follow the Israelite soldiers.

At this moment, Joshua gave the signal by stretching out his javelin, and the soldiers who were in ambush rose up and easily conquered the empty city. The soldiers in two different groups attacked the soldiers of Ai and destroyed them completely.

The Lesson Given in the Conquering of Ai

We can learn a couple of important things from the process involved in the conquering of the city of Ai. The first is that we have to know the will of God in everything.

They shouldn't have just thought, "Two or three thousand soldiers are enough because it's a small city," but asked God what to do. Until the moment they conquered all the lands in Canaan, they had to ask for God's power with humble hearts and minds.

Essentially, when we plan something and try to accomplish it, we first have to hear the voice of the Holy Spirit and be guided by Him through fervent prayers to discern the will of God.

Also, for us to walk with God, we have to cast off sins and evil completely and become sanctified. The reason why Israel lost at Ai the first time is not because the people of Ai were big and strong. It was because God was not with them because of the sin of Achan. Only after they removed this sin from Israel could they win by the help of God.

One of the common mistakes that men make is that we are so keen to achieve some works of God that we sometimes do not discern the will of God, which is the most important thing.

1 Thessalonians 4:3 says, *"For this is the will of God, your sanctification."* But for the Israelites at that time, they thought the important thing was to quickly attack the city of Ai and conquer it. But what is the most important to God is that the people of Israel depart from sins and keep their holiness as God's elect.

It's the same today. Even though we work so much for God's kingdom, we constantly have to check our words and deeds to cast off sins, so that we can pursue peace with everyone and achieve sanctification.

When we cleanse our hearts and receive the guidance of the Holy Spirit to obey what God really wants, only then can we harvest good and abundant fruit in all things and give glory to God.

Proclamation on Mount Gerizim and Mount Ebal

Joshua did not just keep on marching to conquer the rest of the Canaan Land but before God with the people he built an altar. This was a part of the last will of Moses.

See, I am setting before you today a blessing and a curse: the blessing, if you listen to the commandments of the LORD your God, which I am commanding you today; and the curse, if you do not listen to the commandments of the LORD your God, but turn aside from the way which I am commanding you today, by following other gods which you have not known. It shall come about, when the LORD your God brings you into the land where you are entering to possess it, that you shall place the blessing on Mount Gerizim and the curse on Mount Ebal (Deuteronomy 11:26-29).

At the center of the Canaan Land, there were two mountains. One was called Gerizim and the other was Ebal. Moses asked Joshua to proclaim the commandments of God to the people once again at this place.

Since they had gone through a defeat because of the sin of Achan, Joshua probably felt the need to once again teach God's Law to the people that had been delivered to them by Moses.

Joshua built the altar, divided the Israel into two, and let each group stand before the Mount Gerizim and Ebal. And the Levites began to proclaim the Law of God to the people with loud voice.

When the words of blessing were proclaimed, those people of the tribes of Simeon, Levi, Judah, Issachar, Joseph, and Benjamin who were standing at Mount Gerizim responded with "Amen," and for the curses, the people of the tribes of Reuben, Gad, Asher, Zebulun, Dan, and Naphtali responded with "Amen" at Mount Ebal.

Can you imagine what kind of impact this had on the hearts of the sons of Israel? Millions of people stood in two groups, the Law of God was solemnly proclaimed, and the people responded to both blessings and curses with 'Amen.'

Those who attended this sedate ceremony probably remembered the commands of God and had no desire to violate them 'until their deaths.' Especially, they experienced so clearly, through the defeat at Ai, what kind of blessings and curses they would experience according to their obedience or disobedience to the word of God.

They were taught the word of God so many times by Moses, and now Joshua could just speak it once again. But God made it so dramatic that the people could keep the Law deep in their hearts.

We can never over-emphasize the importance of the Law of God. Even though they learned the Law of God again and again, they sometimes left God and committed sins and consequently suffered from famine, wars, and suppression from other countries. Time and time again they repented and sought God in times of hardship, but when they had peace, they violated the Law again.

But if we receive the solutions to our problems and dwell in sins again, the Bible tells us, that we will suffer something greater than before. After Jesus healed a paralytic, He wanted him not to sin any more (John 5:14). 2 Peter 2:20 also says, *"For if, after they have escaped the defilements of the world by the knowledge of the Lord and Savior Jesus Christ, they are again entangled in them and are overcome, the last state has become worse for them than the first."*

What God desires from His children is not forced belief just to avoid sufferings or calamities. He wants true children who understand the heart of God, keep His commands with joy and thanks for His love, and sanctify themselves to resemble God Himself.

Chapter 9

The Sun and the Moon Stand Still

- Victory of the Battle of Gibeon -

Joshua 10:12-14

Then Joshua spoke to the LORD in the day when the LORD delivered up the Amorites before the sons of Israel, and he said in the sight of Israel, "O sun, stand still at Gibeon, And O moon in the valley of Aijalon." So the sun stood still, and the moon stopped, Until the nation avenged themselves of their enemies. Is it not written in the book of Jashar? And the sun stopped in the middle of the sky and did not hasten to go down for about a whole day. There was no day like that before it or after it, when the LORD listened to the voice of a man; for the LORD fought for Israel.

At the time when Israel was entering into the Canaan Land, there were seven major local tribes that had settled on the lands. They were the Canaanites, the Hittites, the Hivites, the Perizzites, the Girgashites, the Amorites, and the Jebusites.

The Girgashites were relatively weaker than the others and they were later integrated into other tribes. So, sometimes, the Bible mentions only six tribes leaving out the Girgashite. Additionally, there were Philistines, Amalekites, and Kenites who were around the Canaan Land.

When the city of Ai which was located in the central part of Canaan was conquered, those different peoples in Canaan were afraid and tried to find a solution. The Hittite, Amorite, Canaanite, Hivite, and Jebusite agreed that they would form a united force to fight the nation of Israel.

But another tribe tried a different method.

Lies of Gibeon to Have Peace Treaty

One day some strangers came to the camp of Israel wanting

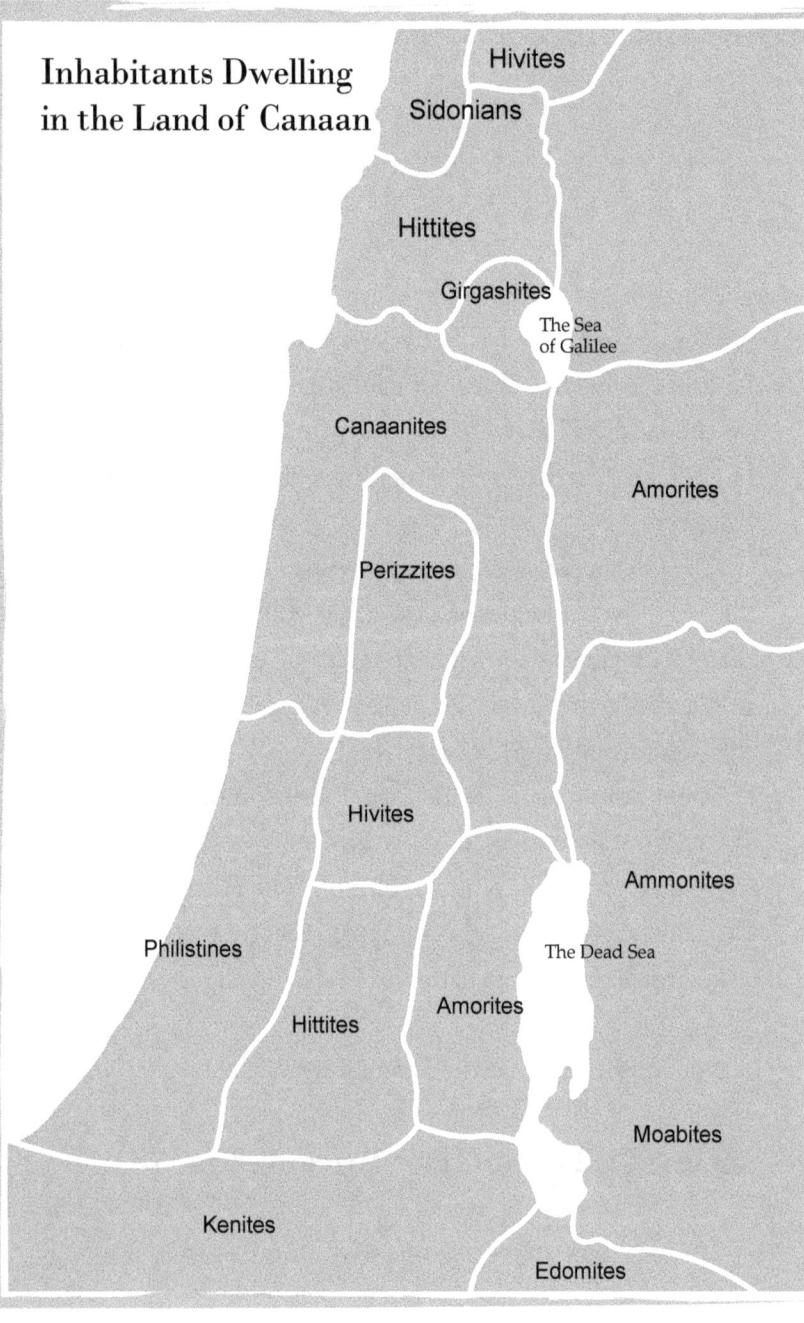

to establish a covenant of peace with them. The Israelites were cautious of them and asked them a question.

> *The men of Israel said to the Hivites, "Perhaps you are living within our land; how then shall we make a covenant with you?" (Joshua 9:7)*

They said they were from a distant country and they came for a peace treaty upon hearing about the fame of the LORD God, what He had done in Egypt and how He let the Israelites conquer some of the people in Canaan. The Hivites who were dwelling in Gibeon chose to deceive Israel and secure a peace treaty rather than to fight against them.

At that time Hivites were living in two areas: one near the Mt. Hermon to the north and the other at Gibeon in the middle of the Land of Canaan. The Hivites who came for a peace treaty were from the Gibeon. For this reason the Bible sometimes refers to the Hivites as people of Gibeon.

Actually, God commanded the people of Israel not to make any covenants with people in Canaan or show favor to them.

> *When the LORD your God brings you into the land where you are entering to possess it, and clears away many nations before you, the Hittites and the Girgashites and the Amorites and the Canaanites and the Perizzites*

> and the Hivites and the Jebusites, seven nations greater and stronger than you, and when the LORD your God delivers them before you and you defeat them, then you shall utterly destroy them. You shall make no covenant with them and show no favor to them (Deuteronomy 7:1-2).

The reason why God told them not to make any covenants with the people in Canaan was because of the fear that they might also become stained by the sins that prevailed in Canaan. As already mentioned, in Canaan and neighboring lands people would mercilessly burn their own children in sacrifice to their gods and played the harlot.

But if people well distanced from Canaan wanted to have peace with Israel and serve, God said it was OK to have peace with them.

But these people who had come to see Joshua said that they had come from a far off land, the bread they had brought was now dry and crumbling and their clothes, shoes, and wineskins were worn out.

> This our bread was warm when we took it for our provisions out of our houses on the day that we left to come to you; but now behold, it is dry and has become crumbled. These wineskins which we filled were new, and behold, they are torn; and these our clothes and our sandals are worn out because of the very long journey (Joshua 9:12-13).

So, Joshua made the peace treaty with them without asking God or carefully examining the case.

> So the men of Israel took some of their provisions, and did not ask for the counsel of the LORD. Joshua made peace with them and made a covenant with them, to let them live; and the leaders of the congregation swore an oath to them (Joshua 9:14-15).

A mistake was made again similar to when they attacked Ai. They decided what to do just by listening to the reports of the scouts without asking the will of God.

Gibeon was not far from Israel's camp at Gilgal. The dry bread and worn out clothes were all false testimony. Three days later the Israelites came to know the truth that these people were the Hivites dwelling in Gibeon. But, it was after they had already made the covenant.

The consequence was that they had to give the Hivites the lands of Gibeon, which they were supposed to have conquered. Although they were cheated by those people, since they made an oath before God, they couldn't reverse it.

> Why have you deceived us, saying, "We are very far from you," when you are living within our land? (Joshua 9:22)

> So they answered Joshua and said, "Because it was

certainly told your servants that the LORD your God had commanded His servant Moses to give you all the land, and to destroy all the inhabitants of the land before you; therefore we feared greatly for our lives because of you, and have done this thing" (Joshua 9:24).

Because Israel had already made an oath before God, they let them live. But Joshua made them common laborers, 'hewers of wood' and 'drawers of water,' for the congregation and for the altar of the LORD (Joshua 9:27).

Some may say Israel could have called the covenant invalid since the people from Gibeon had deceived them. But any kind of oath made before God must be kept in any case.

It's the same when we make a promise with somebody. Even if that promise is not beneficial for us or even causes us damage, we must keep it. Even if the other person cheated us or deceived us, it is we who allowed ourselves to be cheated or deceived, which means, we should not just break the promise.

Lessons to Be Learned from the Incident with Gibeon

Through the incident at Gibeon we should realize how important it is that anything that we do must be done by first realizing the will of God and then following it.

Though it was not intentional, as a consequence of making peace treaty with people of Gibeon, Israel violated the command of God telling them not to make any covenants with the people in Canaan. If they had only asked the counsel of God, they wouldn't have made this kind of mistake.

In our lives, in our businesses or in contract arrangements, some people may try to cheat us. However, in cases like these we cannot just let them cheat us because the Bible tells us to 'seek the benefit of others' (1 Corinthians 10:24).

Seeking benefits and advantages for others in goodness is one thing, but giving others a benefit while accepting being cheated is something completely different. If we just look at the facts that seem obvious, we may not understand the evil intentions of other people and be deceived and swindled. Also, if we just think about the great benefit we will get, we are apt to believe the lies of others.

Therefore, the important thing is to discern the will of God by asking for His counsel through fervent prayers. If we have only goodness in our hearts and no greed, then we can receive the guidance of the Holy Spirit. This way we gain the wisdom of God and even when another person is trying to cheat us, the Holy Spirit will let us realize it and teach us the way to avoid it

Next, we have to understand how important words that come from our lips are.

Because of the incident with Gibeon, several hundred years after they had made the covenant with them, Israel had to go through a disaster. There was a famine that lasted for three years, and David prayed about it. God said it was because the Israel violated the covenant they had made with people of Gibeon.

Namely, Saul, the first King of Israel, tried to destroy all people of Gibeon thus violating the covenant that Joshua had made with them. As a result there was a famine throughout Israel. Finally, the famine stopped only after they killed seven descendants of Saul as requested by the people of Gibeon.

In Judges chapter 11, there is another person who caused himself such a great agony with the words from his lips. It was Jephthah. When he was about to fight against the sons of Ammon, he made a vow that if God would give him victory, he would offer as a burnt offering the first person who came out to receive him when he got back home.

God does not accept a person as a burnt offering, nor did He tell Jephthah to give any burnt offering. But before the great battle Jephthah made this vow and finally he won the battle against the sons of Ammon.

When he came back home after the victory, his only daughter was first to come to receive him. She came out to meet her father with tambourines and with dancing.

Jephthah said, *"Alas, my daughter! You have brought me very low, and you are among those who trouble me; for I have given my word to the LORD, and I cannot take it back"* (Judges 11:35).

Not only his daughter, but nobody would want to die that way. But Jephthah made a careless vow to sacrifice a human life just to get what he wanted. Because of that, he had to give his only daughter as a burnt offering.

Had he broken his vow by not giving his daughter as a burnt offering, he would have been put into greater hardships and more difficult situations than losing his daughter, through the accusations of Satan. The power of the word is that great; even death and life are in the power of the tongue (Proverbs 18:21).

We should always be careful with our words so that we will not say anything that can cause Satan to bring accusations against us. We have to cast off all useless words like careless vows, words of complaint, words of resentment, negative words, or words of judging and condemnation. Let us only speak words of truth and goodness to please God.

Battles in the Southern Part of Canaan

Gibeon was a busy city, like one of the royal cities, and all its men were mighty. It was this city of Gibeon that entered into a peace treaty with Israel just to survive. This news shocked the other people in Canaan and made them tremble. Also, since there was no opposition in the Gibeon area, the army of Israel could march on more quickly.

So, the five kings of the Amorites that dwelled around Gibeon formed an ally and attacked Gibeon, because Gibeon was like a traitor in their sight. Since the people of Gibeon couldn't overcome the allied forces, they asked Israel for help.

Come up to us quickly and save us and help us, for all

the kings of the Amorites that live in the hill country have assembled against us (Joshua 10:6).

As some say, 'a crisis for one is an opportunity for another,' the allied forces of the Amorites could be a big problem to Israel, but at the same time it could also be a great opportunity. To attack the cities in Canaan one by one would have taken a long time, but if they destroyed the allied forces, they could gain many cities at one time.

The LORD said to Joshua, "Do not fear them, for I have given them into your hands; not one of them shall stand before you" (Joshua 10:8).

When Gibeon asked for help, God said He was with Israel. So, they moved quickly overnight and launched a surprise attack against the Amorite kings. The allied armies of the Amorites were unable to retaliate and were defeated. They began to run away and Israel chased after them.

At this moment, God did something amazing for the Israelites. As the Amorites were running away from Gibeon and while they were on the descent of Beth-horon, large hail stones began to fall on them from heaven.

When these things fall from heaven they will have the force of acceleration, and though large they have little frictional resistance and possess great destructive power. Not only taking people's lives, but they can also destroy buildings.

> *As they fled from before Israel, while they were at the descent of Beth-horon, the LORD threw large stones from heaven on them as far as Azekah, and they died; there were more who died from the hailstones than those whom the sons of Israel killed with the sword (Joshua 10:11).*

This of itself was something truly amazing, but they couldn't just stand by in amazement. They had to chase after the remaining enemy force. If the night came, it would be easy for them to hide, so they had to quickly finish the battle while the sun was up.

The Miracle of Sun and Moon Standing Still

It was almost dusk, and they could see the moon in the eastern sky. At that moment, Joshua showed great faith to fulfill God's command.

> *Then Joshua spoke to the LORD in the day when the LORD delivered up the Amorites before the sons of Israel, and he said in the sight of Israel, "O sun, stand still at Gibeon, and O moon in the valley of Aijalon" (Joshua 10:12).*

What king of this earth can control the sun and the moon? Rather than commanding the sun or the moon, the Amorites were actually serving the sun and the moon as their gods and worshipping them!

But by relying on God who controls everything, Joshua commanded the sun and the moon in the sky to stand still, and God guaranteed his word.

> *So the sun stood still, and the moon stopped, until the nation avenged themselves of their enemies. Is it not written in the book of Jashar? And the sun stopped in the middle of the sky and did not hasten to go down for about a whole day (Joshua 10:13).*

With common human knowledge it is impossible for the sun and the moon to stand still but there is nothing impossible by the power of God the Almighty.

Jesus said to His disciples in Matthew 17:20, *"Because of the littleness of your faith; for truly I say to you, if you have faith the size of a mustard seed, you will say to this mountain, 'Move from here to there,' and it will move; and nothing will be impossible to you."*

Of course, God doesn't just move a mountain or stop the sun and the moon any time He feels like it. He cannot just break the natural laws and order in the universe which is running in perfect harmony through His creation.

But if it is necessary to fulfill the plan of God, and if the children of God show spiritual faith, God can do even greater things than stopping the sun and the moon.

Concerning this battle, Joshua 10:14 says, *"There was no day like that before it or after it, when the LORD listened to the voice of a man; for the LORD fought for Israel."*

Joshua and Israel very quickly conquered Makkedah, Libnah, Lachish, Eglon, Hebron, and Debir, which were in the southern part of Canaan.

> *Joshua struck them from Kadesh-barnea even as far as Gaza, and all the country of Goshen even as far as Gibeon. Joshua captured all these kings and their lands at one time, because the LORD, the God of Israel, fought for Israel (Joshua 10:41-42).*

When Joshua used his own thoughts and put his own theory into practice, he was deceived and he made mistakes. But, when he asked for the counsel of God and obeyed His will, he could even manifest the awesome work of stopping the sun and the moon.

Likewise, if we also look up to the almighty God alone and march on with faith and with positive confessions of faith, we can be guided to prosperity. As Jesus promises in Mark 9:23 *"'If You can?' All things are possible to him who believes,"* unimaginable works of God can take place through us.

I hope we will all arm ourselves with prayer and the word to discern the will of God and obey it so that we can always glorify God in our lives.

Chapter 10

"Give Me This Hill Country"

- Devotion of Caleb -

Joshua 14:10-12

Now behold, the LORD has let me live, just as He spoke, these forty-five years, from the time that the LORD spoke this word to Moses, when Israel walked in the wilderness; and now behold, I am eighty-five years old today. I am still as strong today as I was in the day Moses sent me; as my strength was then, so my strength is now, for war and for going out and coming in. Now then, give me this hill country about which the LORD spoke on that day, for you heard on that day that Anakim were there, with great fortified cities; perhaps the LORD will be with me, and I will drive them out as the LORD has spoken.

In the process of going through so many varied things, Joshua and the sons of Israel increased their faith and continued the conquest of the Land of Canaan. After the battles in central part including Jericho, they defeated the allied forces of the kings in the southern part. But they still had to prepare for more battles.

The news that Israel had conquered the southern portion of Canaan by the power of God spread quickly to the people in the northern part. How surprised the Canaanites must have been!

Now they felt a great need among themselves to unite in a stand against Israel. Among the leaders was King Jabin of Hazor. Hazor was one of the strongest of the cities. The king sent his messengers to his neighboring countries and formed an allied force against Israel.

Battles in the Northern Part of Canaan

Jobab king of Madon; the king of Shimron; the king of Achshaph; the kings who were of the north in the hill country, and in the Arabah—south of Chinneroth, and in the lowland and on the heights of Dor on the west; the Canaanite on the east and on the west, and the Amorite and the Hittite and the Perizzite and the Jebusite in the hill country; and the Hivite at the foot of Hermon in the land of Mizpeh formed an allied force (Joshua 11:1-3).

When they all came out with their armies, their number was like sand on a beach. There were also many horses and chariots, too. The nation of Israel had wandered in the wilderness for a long time and they had now also fought many battles. They had to stand alone against the allied force. They might have been discouraged and fearful if they had relied on their soldiers and strength.

But this time too, God promised them a victory and encouraged Joshua.

Then the LORD said to Joshua, "Do not be afraid because of them, for tomorrow at this time I will deliver all of them slain before Israel; you shall hamstring their horses and burn their chariots with fire" (Joshua 11:6).

With the promise of victory, Joshua and army of the nation of Israel launched a surprise attack without any hesitation as soon as they received the word of God. If Israel had hesitated looking at the reality, they couldn't have advanced so boldly.

The allied forces had camped near the water, and though they believed in their military power, they were thrown into great confusion. Although Israel was outnumbered, the allied army was no match for the Israelites for God was with them. Israel defeated the allied armies of Canaanites all at one time without leaving any survivors. As God commanded, they hamstringed their horses and burned their chariots with fire.

Also, they burned the great city Hazor, which functioned as a unified command center for the allied forces. It was to let them know that it was the punishment of God. They then also conquered other cities one by one. This is how they finished another great battle.

Continuing victories in the central and southern parts of the Canaan Land, they went on to conquer the northern part, and it was the end of a significant chapter of the conquest of Canaan. It was the moment when Israel took the Canaan Land that God had promised them.

> *So Joshua took the whole land, according to all that the LORD had spoken to Moses, and Joshua gave it for an inheritance to Israel according to their divisions by their tribes. Thus the land had rest from war (Joshua 11:23).*

The Fulfillment of God's Promise for the Land of Canaan

It had taken a long time for this day to come. God promised Abraham that He would give them the Canaan Land. But hundreds of years had passed until, finally at the time of Moses, a glimpse of the fulfillment of the promise became visible. Even after the Exodus, there was forty years of life in wilderness and more than seven years of warfare under Joshua before this promise was completely fulfilled.

God promised them that He would give them the land flowing with milk and honey, but there was a condition. Only those who believed and obeyed could receive the blessings of the promise of God.

For example, Exodus 15:26 says, *"And [the LORD] said, 'If you will give earnest heed to the voice of the LORD your God, and do what is right in His sight, and give ear to His commandments, and keep all His statutes, I will put none of the diseases on you which I have put on the Egyptians.'"*

We have to give earnest heed to the voice of the LORD God, do what is right in His sight, give ear to His commandments, and keep all His statutes for us to have no involvement with diseases whatsoever. A person must meet the measure of faith of these conditions for the promise of God to be fulfilled.

For the sons of Israel to enter into the Canaan Land, they also had to have faith, and for them to meet and hold to these conditions, God showed them numerous signs and wonders.

Nevertheless, the first generation of the Exodus did not have faith and all of them except Joshua and Caleb died in the wilderness. The fulfillment of God's promise had to be postponed.

But the second generation of the Exodus was different. They had sure faith in God and obeyed Him together with

Joshua. Finally, they could take the land flowing with milk and honey.

> *Just as the LORD had commanded Moses his servant, so Moses commanded Joshua, and so Joshua did; he left nothing undone of all that the LORD had commanded Moses (Joshua 11:15).*

Joshua was the successor to Moses. He showed absolute trust in and complete obedience to God. Also, the sons of Israel followed Joshua, so that the promise of God could be fulfilled.

Conquering the Land by Each Tribe

But conquering the Canaan Land did not mean their work was all finished. Israel took over the Canaan Land in general, but not all the peoples living in the land were destroyed. They still had to drive away some people in different parts of the land, and they had to settle down to make the land completely their own.

When we look into the history, conquering another country physically does not mean all the battles are completely over and there is peace. Many times there are still some people in different corners who try to recover their land.

Joshua was now old and there still was a lot more land to take, and God made the courses of battles completely different.

God commanded him to distribute the land to all tribes of Israel, not only the parts already conquered but also other parts of the land that still had to be conquered. Until now, all tribes of Israel fought the battles as one but from that time on, each tribe of Israel had to conquer the land that was given to them.

So, the task of taking control of their land was now up to the faith of each individual tribe of Israel. The results would be different according to how much spiritual faith they showed and how much they obeyed the will of God.

And at this moment, one person stood up and asked for his right prior to all other tribes. It was Caleb, the son of Jephunneh.

The Faith and Devotion of Caleb

After they escaped Egypt, the Israelites sent twelve spies to spy out the Canaan Land at Kadesh-barnea. But only two of them made positive professions of faith.

The first generation of the Exodus had witnessed so many great works of God's power, but just because of some negative reports of the ten spies they complained against God. They all died in the wilderness and only two men could go into the Promised Land.

One of them was Joshua, the leader of the second generation of the Exodus, and the other was Caleb.

But My servant Caleb, because he has had a different spirit and has followed Me fully, I will bring into the land which he entered, and his descendants shall take possession of it (Numbers 14:24).

Caleb never forgot God's promise given to him while he was going through the forty years in the wilderness together with all the sons of Israel. He did not forget even as he was fighting the many battles in Canaan for seven years.

One may forget some promises as time passes, but Caleb never forgot God's promise made to him. For more than forty years he always prayed about it.

And when the time came to distribute the Canaan Land, he mentioned God's promise given to him and asked Joshua to give him the land.

What Caleb asked was not as though he wanted to gain something by mentioning all that he had done right. He was not saying that he deserved to receive something because he had been one of the leaders of Israel along with Joshua, and because of all the many meritorious things he had done in the battles he had fought.

It was rather a confession of his faith that had become firmer during the course of forty years of trial. It was expression of his devotion that he would dedicate himself first.

The cave of Machpelah where Abraham, Sarah, Isaac, and

Jacob were buried was in the land of Hebron that he asked to receive. It was a very important place for them. Also, it was the land where the twelve spies of Israel had gone. Furthermore, it was still occupied by the Anakim, and they had to fight to take the land.

The Anakim were strong people. They are the ones the ten spies in the past described as recorded, *"Nephilim (the sons of Anak are part of the Nephilim); and we became like grasshoppers in our own sight, and so we were in their sight"* (Numbers 13:33). Caleb did not ask for a land that was already conquered and safe. He asked for the land of Hebron that God had promised to give to him, although he had to go through difficult battles all over again to take it.

> *Now behold, the LORD has let me live, just as He spoke, these forty-five years, from the time that the LORD spoke this word to Moses, when Israel walked in the wilderness; and now behold, I am eighty-five years old today. I am still as strong today as I was in the day Moses sent me; as my strength was then, so my strength is now, for war and for going out and coming in. Now then, give me this hill country about which the LORD spoke on that day, for you heard on that day that Anakim were there, with great fortified cities; perhaps the LORD will be with me, and I will drive them out as the LORD has spoken (Joshua 14:10-12).*

When he was selected as one of the scouts and he stepped on the blessed land with great vines, figs, and pomegranates covering the landscape, he must have had a different kind of heart from others. Also, he couldn't hold up his righteous indignation when he saw the other spies were making negative reports at Kadesh-barnea. He said, "Why would you oppose God! God is with us!" and he cried tearing his clothes, but his shout couldn't be heard because of the complaining cries of the people.

He had to go through the long period of suffering because of the people who disobeyed God, but all the way through he kept in his heart the images of the land flowing with milk and honey. He was now old, but he kept the promise of God in his heart throughout all the forty years. That is why he wanted to take the land of Hebron, which had mountainous landscape and was difficult to conquer, to ease the burden of Joshua.

What would Joshua have felt at this moment? Caleb was his greatest colleague and friend in faith. He had been with him since the Exodus. He was also one of the elders in Israel now, and he deserved to be respected and rewarded. Thus, when Joshua heard that Caleb wanted to go to the mountainous area where even young warriors did not want to go, he must have at least hesitated to let him do so.

On another side though, he must have been touched by Caleb's attitude trying to fulfill the word of God by taking his portion. Joshua understood Caleb better than anybody else, and as God promised he gave him the land of Hebron. Caleb defeated the big Anakim and took the fertile land as his portion that would last throughout generations. This way he showed an example of faith before the people of Israel. The distribution of the land began this way, beginning with Caleb.

Chapter 11

"It Shall Be Yours"

- Distribution of the Canaan Land -

Joshua 17:15-18

Joshua said to them, "If you are a numerous people, go up to the forest and clear a place for yourself there in the land of the Perizzites and of the Rephaim, since the hill country of Ephraim is too narrow for you." The sons of Joseph said, "The hill country is not enough for us, and all the Canaanites who live in the valley land have chariots of iron, both those who are in Beth-shean and its towns and those who are in the valley of Jezreel." Joshua spoke to the house of Joseph, to Ephraim and Manasseh, saying, "You are a numerous people and have great power; you shall not have one lot only, but the hill country shall be yours. For though it is a forest, you shall clear it, and to its farthest borders it shall be yours; for you shall drive out the Canaanites, even though they have chariots of iron and though they are strong."

For the Israelites, the distribution of the allotments of the lands of their inheritance had a very important meaning. They suffered slavery in Egypt for 400 years, wandered around in the wilderness for forty years, and then went through seven years of difficult warfare. After all this they were receiving the fruits of it. Now they were getting a homeland where they could live in peace with their families.

Exceptions in Distribution of the Inheritance

Each tribe of Israel went before God and received the land in the west of Jordan River as their inheritance, with a couple of exceptions.

First, Reuben, Gad, and half of Manasseh had already received their inheritance before they crossed the Jordan. The lands to east of the Jordan were suitable to raise their livestock, and they asked Moses to give the land to them.

Of course, they promised that they would participate in the conquest of the rest of the Canaan Land in the lands west of the Jordan. They made an oath that they would fight in the front line and wouldn't go back to their houses until all tribes of Israel had received their inheritances.

> *The sons of Gad and the sons of Reuben said, "If we have found favor in your sight, let this land be given to your servants as a possession; do not take us across the Jordan" (Numbers 32:5).*

> *But we ourselves will be armed ready to go before the sons of Israel, until we have brought them to their place, while our little ones live in the fortified cities because of the inhabitants of the land. We will not return to our homes until every one of the sons of Israel has possessed his inheritance (Numbers 32: 17-18).*

Leaving their families, cattle, and possessions east of the Jordan, men who could fight in the war crossed the Jordan and fought in the forefront of battle with the sons of Israel until the conquest was over. When the warfare ended, they were able to return to their inheritance in the lands east of Jordan.

Also, among the twelve tribes, the Levites did not receive any inheritance of land for they were priests of God. But the tribe of Joseph was more prosperous than other tribes by the blessing of God, and the descendants of Joseph's two sons Ephraim and Manasseh received their individual inheritances respectively.

In conclusion, the Levites were excluded, two and a half tribes received their inheritances in the lands east of Jordan, and nine and a half tribes received their inheritances to the west of Jordan. About the method of allotting and distribution of the lands, God had already given the principle to Moses.

> *To the larger group you shall increase their inheritance, and to the smaller group you shall diminish their inheritance; each shall be given their inheritance according to those who were numbered of them. But the land shall be divided by lot. They shall receive their inheritance according to the names of the tribes of their fathers (Numbers 26:54-55).*

The area of the land given to each tribe was decided by the number of people, but they had to decide which part of the land to be given by lots. It was the fairest method so that there wouldn't be any conflicts among the tribes. By casting lots they had the same probability of receiving the good lands.

Also, the sons of Israel had faith that the result of the lot is not coincidence, but it was the will of God (Proverbs 16:33). When Achan committed a sin, they found him among more than two million people by casting lots.

Distribution of the Land among the Twelve Tribes

Complaints and Words of Unbelief of the Tribe of Joseph

But there was a problem while they were distributing the land by casting lots. The tribe of Joseph demanded that they should receive a greater inheritance than the other tribes for they became two tribes by the blessing of God.

> *Then the sons of Joseph spoke to Joshua, saying, "Why have you given me only one lot and one portion for an inheritance, since I am a numerous people whom the LORD has thus far blessed?" (Joshua 17:14)*

In fact the inheritance given to them was not small compared to the other tribes. It was a wide expanse of fertile land in the central part of Canaan. Still, they were complaining that they ought to receive more of an inheritance than they did.

Joshua said to them, *"If you are a numerous people, go up to the forest and clear a place for yourself there in the land of the Perizzites and of the Rephaim, since the hill country of Ephraim is too narrow for you"* (Joshua 17:15). Essentially he told them that if they didn't have enough area to cultivate, they had to enlarge their area by clearing a larger place for themselves.

But again this time, the sons of Joseph did not obey. They

said that even if they cleared the forest their inheritance was still too small for them. They demanded more of the good land. They wanted to gain something good without working to earn it. They also wanted to be served because now they were such a great tribe.

Since they had been blessed by God to become a great tribe, they were supposed to lead the other tribes as Caleb had done to conquer and subjugate the lands that were difficult to conquer. But despite everything, they just complained without taking the initiative to do anything.

> *The sons of Joseph said, "The hill country is not enough for us, and all the Canaanites who live in the valley land have chariots of iron, both those who are in Beth-shean and its towns and those who are in the valley of Jezreel" (Joshua 17:16).*

Furthermore, they made a profession of their lack of faith by saying the people living in the land they had to conquer had chariots of iron. They already forgot why they had to go through the trial in the wilderness for forty years.

Their conquests under Joshua's leadership were a series of miracles. They were never able to physically match their enemies, but they defeated all of them by the power of God. Not just their chariots of iron, but no matter what kinds of weapons their enemies had, they didn't have to be afraid at all if they believed the almighty God.

They had been obeying in all kinds of dangerous situations, but suddenly they became afraid when Joshua told them to conquer their inheritance on their own.

Joshua kept on asking them to show their faith while pointing out their wrong ideas. He advised them that they would be able to enlarge their inheritance by the blessing of God if they showed their faith.

But the sons of Joseph would not obey Joshua's words. They were not able to completely drive out all the Canaanites living in their inheritance (Joshua 16:10, 17:12-13). As a result, they had to suffer continuously.

Whenever Israel became weaker, the Gentiles soon attacked Israel.

But a bigger problem was that Israel came in contact with the Gentile culture that was prohibited by God and they committed sins that caused the anger of God to be aroused. They brought difficult situations repeatedly upon themselves because they did not obey the commands of God with sure faith.

The almighty God who was with Joshua was not only the God of Joshua, but also of Israel. Only if they showed their faith God could show them the same kind of works that He showed through Joshua. God wanted all sons of Israel to have brave and strong faith like Joshua.

The Inheritance of Joshua and Levites

All other tribes except the Levites had received the lands as their inheritance both west and east of the Jordan, but Joshua had not received any of his inheritance yet. He was a powerful servant of God and the leader of all Israel, but he received his inheritance last.

Especially, the inheritance that he received was near the Timnath-serah in the hill country of Ephraim. It was so desolate a land that he had to build the city again (Joshua 19:49-50).

He was a man of brave and strong faith, and he was in a position to be served first. But he served others and made concessions instead. That is why he had been acknowledged by God and became the successor to Moses.

After all tribes received their inheritance, Levites came before Joshua and received their portion. But unlike other tribes, they did not receive any land as their inheritance.

Numbers 18:20 says, *"Then the LORD said to Aaron, 'You shall have no inheritance in their land nor own any portion among them; I am your portion and your inheritance among the sons of Israel.'"* As said, Levites' inheritance and portion was God Himself.

Levites had the duty of giving sacrifices to God and keeping the tabernacle of the LORD. They also had the duty to teach the ordinances and Law of God to the people (Deuteronomy 33:10).

God Himself became their inheritance so that they would not stain their heart with the worldly things but concentrate on serving God. Namely, rather than giving them the land to get a harvest from it, God let them make their living through the tithes and various offerings that the people gave to God.

Levites in today's sense are the pastors and full-time workers who serve the church. Even today, as is the case with those who work in the church, especially the pastors cannot just become pastors or quit as they want.

All pastors are servants of God and they have to offer all their lives to God. Therefore, they should not have worldly jobs or do business with their desires for the world. They should concentrate on the works of God because their only inheritance is God Himself. And to let the pastors do this, the church and the church members have to support the pastors.

Though Levites did not receive land as their inheritance, they still received various cities in which to dwell and use the fields to feed their livestock. They received cities among each tribe of Israel, and this way they lived among all tribes of Israel.

As a result, in any of the allotted areas in Israel, they had a city of Levites. This means each tribe could listen to the word of God and learn it from the Levites who were in close proximity to them. In this way God had arranged for the people of the nation of Israel to stay close to the commandments of God all the time.

Chapter 12

"As for Me and My House, We Will Serve the LORD"

- The Last Will of Joshua -

Joshua 24:14-15

Now, therefore, fear the LORD and serve Him in sincerity and truth; and put away the gods which your fathers served beyond the River and in Egypt, and serve the LORD. If it is disagreeable in your sight to serve the LORD, choose for yourselves today whom you will serve: whether the gods which your fathers served which were beyond the River, or the gods of the Amorites in whose land you are living; but as for me and my house, we will serve the LORD.

After seven years of warfare, Joshua defeated all of the Canaanite kings and conquered many cities in the Canaan Land, but not all Canaanites were driven out. There still were many Canaanites scattered about the land, and some of them even tried to oppose Israel with their chariots of iron.

Of course, the power of God could have driven them out immediately, but God guided the Israelites to subjugate Canaan step by step according to the growth of their faith and trust in God. Furthermore, even if they drove out all Canaanites, it was difficult for them to keep all the land before they could completely populate it.

There could be attacks from other people to take the empty land. The land could be barren without any residents, and wild animals could have prevailed. Therefore, God said He would drive the Canaanites out little by little until Israel's power became great enough in number to fill the Land of Canaan.

I will not drive them out before you in a single year, that the land may not become desolate and the beasts of the field become too numerous for you. I will drive them out before you little by little, until you become fruitful and take possession of the land (Exodus 23:29-30).

Even though it would take a long period of time to fulfill this, each tribe of Israel had to fight and drive out the Canaanites who still remained in the allotments of their inheritance.

God gave the inheritance of the lands to each tribe and told them to take it, and He promised that He would drive out the Canaanites no matter how strong they were. It's just that the result would be different according to how faithfully the nation of Israel believed the promise of God and acted according to it.

The Farewell Address of the Leader Joshua

Each tribe that received inheritance respectively began to take their land according to their faith and strength. Based on what they had learned from Joshua, some of them asked for God's counsel or had some personal strategies to advance into the Canaan Land more and more.

A lot of time passed and Joshua knew that he was old and the remainder of his time was short before his death. He now felt the need to remind the Israelites of the promise of God once again so they could reaffirm their faith. Just like Moses did when he was going back to God, Joshua called for all Israel to gather, for their elders and their heads and their judges and their officers, and gave his final words of advice.

His farewell address is written from Joshua 23:1 onward. In summation, he was telling them to keep the commands of God, stay near Him, and love Him without change of mind.

> *Be very firm, then, to keep and do all that is written in the book of the law of Moses, so that you may not turn aside from it to the right hand or to the left, so that you will not associate with these nations, these which remain among you, or mention the name of their gods, or make anyone swear by them, or serve them, or bow down to them. But you are to cling to the LORD your God, as you have done to this day (Joshua 23:6-8).*

Until that time God was with Joshua and gave Israel amazing victories. God promised that He would defeat any enemy, no matter how strong, and give the nation of Israel the whole land of Canaan if Israel loved God, clung to Him, and kept His commandments.

> *One of your men puts to flight a thousand, for the LORD your God is He who fights for you, just as He promised you. So take diligent heed to yourselves to love the LORD your God (Joshua 23:10-11).*

Joshua also reminded them once again concerning associating

with the Gentiles and the consequences of backsliding in faith, forgetting the promise of God, and worshipping idols.

> *For if you ever go back and cling to the rest of these nations, these which remain among you, and intermarry with them, so that you associate with them and they with you, know with certainty that the LORD your God will not continue to drive these nations out from before you; but they will be a snare and a trap to you, and a whip on your sides and thorns in your eyes, until you perish from off this good land which the LORD your God has given you (Joshua 23:12-13).*

A Time of Solemn Resolution at Shechem

Joshua finally gathered the people at Shechem, between Mount Ebal and Mount Gerizim where they proclaimed the words of blessings and curses, to have a time of solemn resolution.

First, Joshua reminded them of the faithfulness of God who fulfilled His promise that He gave to Abraham, and the almightiness of God who defeated the strength of Egypt and seven tribes of Canaan.

If serving the LORD God did not seem right in their sight, then he asked them to choose which god they would serve. He demanded of them once again to fear God alone and serve Him in sincerity and truth (Joshua 24:2-14).

Joshua called for their determination to cast away all idols and faithfully keep only the commandments of God.

> *If it is disagreeable in your sight to serve the LORD, choose for yourselves today whom you will serve: whether the gods which your fathers served which were beyond the River, or the gods of the Amorites in whose land you are living; but as for me and my house, we will serve the LORD. The people answered and said, "Far be it from us that we should forsake the LORD to serve other gods." Joshua said to the people, "You are witnesses against yourselves that you have chosen for yourselves the LORD, to serve Him." And they said, "We are witnesses" (Joshua 24:15-16, 22).*

As Joshua firmly said, "As for me and my house, we will serve the LORD," the sons of Israel also did not hesitate to vow once again, "We will serve the LORD our God and we will obey His voice."

> *So Joshua made a covenant with the people that day, and made for them a statute and an ordinance in Shechem (Joshua 24:25).*

After Joshua confirmed the covenant, he once again taught them the commands of God to serve the LORD. He took a large stone and set it up as evidence. Then he dismissed the people, each to his inheritance. After this, Joshua quietly ended his life of fervent passion and faith, at the age of 110.

Epilogue
– Conquering the Land Flowing with Milk and Honey –

The Conquest by Faith, Obedience, and Devotion

Until now we have looked into the process of the people of Israel going into the Promised Land of Canaan. God made a great nation from one person, and we can see each step of this process is so precise and accurate.

The history of conquering the Canaan Land is written in detail in the five books of Exodus, Leviticus, Numbers, Deuteronomy, and Joshua. Exodus writes about the birth of Moses and the beginning of the Exodus from Egypt. The book of Leviticus contains the heart of God who wants His children to be holy and sanctified.

The book of Numbers writes about the endurance of God who bore with the people even when they were disobedient and rebellious in the wilderness. Deuteronomy contains the sermon of Moses who preached the word of God at three different times at the plain of Moab. Lastly, the book of Joshua contains the history of the second generation of Exodus conquering the Canaan Land with Joshua, the successor to Moses.

If the history of conquering Canaan can be put into one phrase, it is, 'By faith, obedience, and devotion.' They could gain the Canaan Land when they looked at it and marched on toward it with faith.

Joshua and Caleb believed the promise of God and devoted themselves with all their life. Their act originated from faith and obedience. In that process, God wanted the sons of Israel to be holy and sanctified. The sanctification movement is seen repeatedly in the steps towards the Canaan Land.

When God first called Moses, He told him to remove his shoes. This spiritually symbolizes that he had to cast away sins and evil. When God gave His Law to the people through Moses, He first had them sanctify themselves.

When they were about to cross the Jordan River, God

made them sanctify themselves. They had to circumcise themselves just before the battle against the city of Jericho. God wants to have sanctified children, and God can walk with them only when they are sanctified.

> *Therefore you are to be perfect, as your heavenly Father is perfect (Matthew 5:48).*

> *Like the Holy One who called you, be holy yourselves also in all your behavior; because it is written, "You shall be holy, for I am holy" (1 Peter 1:15-16).*

Conquering Canaan Is the Model of a Journey of Faith

Then, what is the reason that five books among the sixty-six books of the Bible record the history about Israel conquering the Canaan Land? It's because the conquering of the Land of Canaan is a model that represents the journey of our faith.

For the sons of Israel who just came out of Egypt, God

parted the Red Sea and gave them water from a rock from His side. But as time passed, God began to require of them their own faith. Namely, when they were crossing the Jordan River, God told them that the priests had to carry the ark of the covenant and step into the River.

When they conquered the strong city of Jericho, God told them to march around the city once a day for six days. Then they were to march around seven times on the seventh day, and shout with loud voice. This was to see their faith and obedience. The process in which each tribe received their inheritance shows that God works according to the measure of our faith as we grow up in spirit.

The life on earth is the life of a sojourner. It's a continuation of battles against the ruler of darkness and the evil spirits in the air. Even if we have received blessings, we have to make our walk firm, and when we accomplish something we have to accomplish the next thing. This process will go on until we get to the heavenly kingdom.

Even today, God gives us many promises of blessings in the

Bible. The Lord Jesus also promised us that He would prepare a dwelling place in heaven and come back to get us. Therefore, anyone who believes the word of God in the Bible and acts with faith will be guided to the prosperous and blessed way. He will also receive a beautiful dwelling place in the heavenly kingdom.

Therefore, even if there are obstacles in front of us, we have to have an unchanging heart to believe in and trust in God completely without being shaken at all, like Joshua and Caleb.

Once God's promise is given, we should believe it until the end. We should not grow weary or become lazy in the middle, but march on with faith until we gain substantial fruit.

Hebrews 3:14 says, *"For we have become partakers of Christ, if we hold fast the beginning of our assurance firm until the end."* As said, we should have New Jerusalem as our final goal, and even if we may see our shortcomings and even if there are difficulties in our way, our hope should never change.

I pray in the name of the Lord that God will always guide you to the blessings of milk and honey and eventually let you enjoy eternal blessings in the heavenly kingdom.

About the Author
Dr. Jaerock Lee

Dr. Jaerock Lee was born in Muan, Jeonnam Province, Republic of Korea, in 1943. In his twenties, he suffered from a variety of incurable diseases for seven years and awaited death with no hope for recovery. One day in the spring of 1974, however, he was led to a church by his sister, and when he knelt down to pray, the living God immediately healed him of all his diseases.

From the moment Dr. Lee met the living God through that wonderful experience, he has loved God with all his heart and sincerity, and in 1978 was called to be a servant of God. He prayed fervently so that he could clearly understand the will of God and wholly accomplish it, and obeyed all the word of God. In 1982, he founded Manmin Church in Seoul, S. Korea, and countless works of God, including miraculous healings and wonders, have been taking place at his church.

In 1986, Dr. Lee was ordained as a pastor at the Annual Assembly of Jesus' Sungkyul Church of Korea, and four years later in 1990, his sermons began to be broadcast on the Far East Broadcasting Company, the Asia Broadcast Station, and the Washington Christian Radio System to Australia, Russia, the Philippines, and many more.

Three years later in 1993, Manmin Central Church was selected as one of the "World's Top 50 Churches" by the *Christian World* magazine (US) and he received an Honorary Doctorate of Divinity from Christian Faith College, Florida, USA, and in 1996 a Ph. D. in Ministry from Kingsway Theological Seminary, Iowa, USA.

Since 1993, Dr. Lee has taken the lead in world mission through many overseas crusades in L.A., New York, Baltimore, Hawaii of the USA, Tanzania, Argentina, Uganda, Japan, Pakistan, Kenya, the Philippines,

Honduras, India, Russia, Germany, Peru, and Democratic Republic of Congo, and in 2002 he was called a "worldwide pastor" by major Christian newspapers in Korea for his work in various overseas crusades.

As of August 2009, Manmin Central Church is a congregation of more than 100,000 members and has 9,000 branch churches throughout the globe including 52 domestic branch churches in major cities, and has so far commissioned more than 133 missionaries to 25 countries, including the United States, Russia, Germany, Canada, Japan, China, France, India, Kenya, and many more.

To this day, Dr. Lee has written 57 books, including bestsellers *Tasting Eternal Life before Death*, *My Life My Faith I & II*, *The Way of Salvation*, *The Measure of Faith*, *Heaven I & II*, and *Hell*, and his works have been being translated into more than 41 languages.

His Christian columns appear on *The Hankook Ilbo*, *The JoongAng Daily*, *The Dong-A Ilbo*, *The Munhwa Ilbo*, *The Seoul Shinmun*, *The Kyunghyang Shinmun*, *The Hankyoreh Shinmun*, *The Korea Economic Daily*, *The Korea Herald*, *The Shisa News*, *The Christian Press* and *The Nation Evangelization Newspaper*.

Dr. Lee is currently leader of many missionary organizations and associations including: Chairman, The United Holiness Church of Jesus Christ; Permanent President of the World Christianity Revival Mission Association; President, The Nation Evangelization Newspaper; President, Manmin World Mission; Founder, Manmin TV; Founder & Board Chairman, Global Christian Network (GCN); Founder & Board Chairman, World Christian Doctors Network (WCDN); and Founder & Board Chairman, Manmin International Seminary (MIS).

Other powerful books by the same author

Heaven I & II

A detailed sketch of the gorgeous living environment the heavenly citizens enjoy and beautiful description of different levels of heavenly kingdoms.

The Message of the Cross

A powerful awakening message for all the people who are spiritually asleep! In this book you will find the reason Jesus is the only Savior and the true love of God.

Hell

An earnest message to all mankind from God, who wishes not even one soul to fall into the depths of hell! You will discover the never-before-revealed account of the cruel reality of the Lower Grave and hell.

Tasting Eternal Life Before Death

A testimonial memoirs of Dr. Jaerock Lee, who was born again and saved from the valley of death and has been leading an exemplary Christian life.

The Measure of Faith

What kind of a dwelling place, crown and reward are prepared for you in heaven? This book provides with wisdom and guidance for you to measure your faith and cultivate the best and most mature faith.

Awaken, Israel!

Why has God kept His eyes on Israel from the beginning of the world to this day? What kind of His providence has been prepared for Israel in the last days, who await the Messiah?

My Life My Faith I & II

Dr. Jaerock Lee's autobiography provides the most fragrant spiritual aroma for the readers, through his life extracted from the love of God blossomed in midst of the dark waves, cold yoke and the deepest despair.

The Power of God

A must-read that serves as an essential guide by which one can possess true faith and experience the wondrous power of God

www.urimbooks.com

www.ingramcontent.com/pod-product-compliance
Lightning Source LLC
LaVergne TN
LVHW010318070526
838199LV00065B/5600